The 92nd Infantry Division

and the Italian Campaign in World War II

To Arlene Fox
a woman of quiet dignity
and stupendous elegance

The 92nd Infantry Division

and the Italian Campaign in World War II

Daniel K. Gibran

McFarland & Company, Inc., Publishers
Jefferson, North Carolina, and London

ALSO BY DANIEL K. GIBRAN

*The Falklands War:
Britain Versus the Past in the South Atlantic*
(McFarland, 1997)

Library of Congress Cataloguing-in-Publication Data

Gibran, Daniel K., 1950–
　　The 92nd Infantry Division and the Italian campaign in World
　War II / by Daniel K. Gibran.
　　　　p.　cm.
　　Includes bibliographical references and index.

　　ISBN-13: 978-0-7864-1009-5
　　(softcover : 50# alkaline paper) ∞

　　1. United States. Army. Infantry Division, 92nd — History.
　2. World War, 1939–1945 — Campaigns — Italy.　3. World
　War, 1939–1945 — African Americans.　4. World War, 1939–
　1945 — Regimental histories — United States.　I. Title.

D769.31 92nd .G53　　2001
940.54'1273 — dc21
　　　　　　　　　　　　　　　　　　　　　　2001030380

British Library cataloguing data are available

©2001 Daniel K. Gibran. All rights reserved

*No part of this book may be reproduced or transmitted in any form
or by any means, electronic or mechanical, including photocopying
or recording, or by any information storage and retrieval system,
without permission in writing from the publisher.*

Manufactured in the United States of America

Front cover: The military insignia of the 92nd "Buffalo" Infantry
Division.

McFarland & *Company, Inc., Publishers*
　Box 611, Jefferson, North Carolina 28640
　　www.mcfarlandpub.com

Contents

Preface vii
Introduction 1

1. The 92nd Infantry Division and General Edward Almond: Preparation for War 11
2. Deployment to the War Zone and General Almond's Command 39
3. From Cinquale to Hill X and Massa 71
4. Vernon Baker: A Medal, a Signorina, and a New Life 91
5. Courage Under Fire: The Story of Lieutenant John Fox ... 123
6. The Long Road to Recognition 141
7. Summary and Conclusion 161
8. Epilogue: An Encounter with America 169

Appendix: More Information on the Medal of Honor 177
Notes 183
Bibliography 191
Index 195

Preface

The history of the all–Black 92nd Infantry Division during World War II is a history of human drama and individual courage. On the one hand, it can be viewed as a microhistory of race relations in America, of two major races within the American geography, one visibly dominant and the other obviously subjected, struggling against considerable odds to hammer out and accommodate a working relationship within the rigid strictures of segregation. On the other hand, it is also a history of tactical failures and poor leadership, of strategic blunders and myopic planning, interspersed with individual acts of courage and heroism. Several aspects of this history have been recalled in other books, some describing the day-to-day events of the war in superb detail, others concentrating on tactical maneuvers and battle plans with little or no emphasis on individual failures and triumphs.

This book tells the story of some of those failures and triumphs. It seeks to do so in a dispassionate way, paying particular attention not only to human drama and environmental context, but also to the rigors of historical analysis and objectivity. Against a comprehensive historical and geographical background of conflict in the Mediterranean Theater of Operations, Italy in particular, this story of the 92nd Infantry Division, a division of Black Americans going to war under senior white leadership, unfolds. The dramatis personae in this story are one white and two black men, each playing crucial roles in a military campaign that lasted for less than six months but was characterized by intense fighting against an entrenched enemy. It was a campaign marked by incessant organizational chops and changes, by poor strategic leadership, and by a pervasive atmosphere of distrust and racial undertones. It was also a campaign that brought to the fore some of the best qualities in men, qualities of indomitable courage and intrepidity displayed in acts of heroism.

Far from being a definitive history of the 92nd Infantry Division, this book takes a different cut into that history, using salient aspects of it for background and drama. The story of the white commander who led his troops into battle is recalled here, including an examination of his early life and military preparations for a leadership role of black troops, and more importantly, his human relation skills and strategic focus. It is alleged by many surviving black veterans that among those in leadership roles whose actions and attitudes adversely affected black combat performance during this short campaign, this white commander, Major General Ned Almond, stands without an equal.

The acts of bravery of two black junior officers on the rugged and treacherous terrain of Italy are recalled here without much fanfare. Lieutenant Vernon Baker, one of the heroes of this story, came from humble beginnings, fought with great courage on a dry and steep hillside in Italy in April 1945, came home to the United States, and after fifty years, stood before the president to receive the Medal of Honor. Then he returned to his cottage in St. Maries, Idaho, where he lives in splendid isolation with his German-born wife. His comrade, Lieutenant John Fox, did not make it back to his waiting wife and infant daughter in Massachusetts; he died in the ultimate act of self-sacrifice on a hill nestled in the remote Italian village of Sommocolonia by calling artillery fire on his location. His young, widowed wife never remarried and still cherishes the thought that her loved one whom death has snatched prematurely will return one day.

In recasting these poignant stories, the author has given an account (detailed in the Epilogue) of his own encounter with some of the actors, and the modest role he played in helping to advance a cause held dear by African Americans in this country — a cause that sought fair treatment and justice for black veterans of World War II. That effort, initiated by the Department of Defense and then painstakingly executed by a small group of dedicated and skillful researchers, would culminate in the award of the nation's highest medal for valor in combat when seven blacks received the Medal of Honor on January 13, 1997. In a moving ceremony at the White House on that cold, wintry morning, the author's encounter reached a new height and level of satisfaction in the goodness of this country and all that it stands for.

I must pause here to acknowledge the invaluable assistance I received from a number of individuals during the course of researching and writing this story. First, I owe a great debt of gratitude to Richard Kohn, a military historian of impeccable credentials and penetrating insight, whose advice and care over the years have been a great source of inspiration to me. I have, in numerous ways, benefited from his friendship. Joseph Galloway of *US News and World Report* fame provided me with pages of interview transcripts, and for this I am grateful. A number of World War II veterans from the 92nd Infantry Division, particularly Jehu Hunter and Major Clark, have provided me with many useful insights, shedding light into some of the darker recesses of human relationships and personnel interactions within the division. I thank these brave souls for their continued interest and willingness to help. In particular, I want to thank Vernon Baker and his wife, Heidi, for their hospitality, for allowing us to stay in their home for a week during the course of long interview periods. They both endured mental anguish with a cheerful disposition. And finally, I want to thank Mrs. Arlene Fox, widow of Lieutenant John Fox, and a woman of exceeding charm and grace, for her understanding and recall of a heart-wrenching episode in her life. Amidst tears and laughter, she remained poised and dignified; a remarkable woman and an example of patient endurance Mrs. Fox is. I dedicate this book to her.

INTRODUCTION

Although World War II utilized more Negro manpower than previous military conflicts involving the United States, it represented, nonetheless, a continuation of a trend that went back to pre–Colonial days. Blacks participated in every major war engaged in by this nation. They fought alongside whites in the French and Indian Wars and other pre–Revolutionary continental wars. When bloodshed marked the independence of this country from Britain, a former Negro slave from Boston, Crispus Attucks, became the first man to die in the nation's struggle for freedom. Black participation in the Revolutionary War was a pragmatic response to manpower shortages where the majority fought as infantrymen in integrated units led by whites.

In the War of 1812, soldiers and slaves manned the bulwarks of huge cotton bales and successfully turned the tide of battle. When the Civil War erupted less than fifty years later, tens of thousands of blacks were recruited as laborers, and many served in combat. In all, 186,000 blacks swelled the ranks of the Union Army, many thousands in combat regiments and labor units. The Navy's 30,000 blacks accounted for 25 percent of its overall strength. And during World War I, 404,000 black officers and enlisted men, nearly 11 percent of the Army's strength, served this nation. Thousands served as frontline troops in regiments of the 92nd and 93rd Infantry Divisions in France. In particular, the 369th Infantry Regiment fought continuously for 91 consecutive days, losing many officers and enlisted men. Two of its privates, Henry Johnson and Needham Roberts, were the first American enlisted men to be awarded medals by the French government, and the regiment itself was recognized with the prestigious Croix de Guerre.

But in a departure from other military conflicts in which blacks participated, World War I marked the beginning of an ugly campaign of rumors and innuendoes discrediting Negro soldiers. The litany of criticisms stemmed from a perceived lackluster combat performance by several organic elements of the all-black 92nd Infantry Division. The conviction among senior white leadership was simple: blacks did not perform well in combat and could not be relied upon as effective soldiers.

From the beginning of its formation and subsequent preparation for deployment overseas during World War I, the 92nd Infantry had troubles. Strict racial segregation was practiced, and the facilities set aside for use by black troops were severely limited. Morale among the rank and file was at an all time low, and training was piecemeal and incomplete. The division hurriedly left for France, poorly trained and poorly led.

Commanded by Major General Charles Ballou, the 92nd spent most of the first two months after its arrival in France in a "quiet" sector where it did not participate in any fighting. In September 1918, the division entered combat alongside French troops at the beginning of the Meuse-Argonne Offensive. Lacking internal cohesion and still suffering from low morale, the 92nd Division performed poorly and sluggishly. It was quickly withdrawn and then reorganized before returning to the offensive a month later on November 10 and 11 as part of the U.S. Second Army.

The new division commander, Lieutenant General Robert Bullard, had earlier served with black National Guard troops in the Spanish-American War. Thus he had some familiarity with blacks. During the final days of World War I, one brigade of the division performed well; the others, plagued with a number of internal problems that General Bullard interpreted as "lack of aggression," retreated from battle. Many of the division's organic elements became disorganized, and hundreds of enlisted men and officers including whites, fled in the face of enemy fire.

When the final offensive of this war was launched a few weeks later, the 92nd Infantry Division was withdrawn and its commander relieved. While no official explanation was given at the time, speculations abounded. In the main, they concentrated on the failure of black troops to engage the enemy and fight.

When he published his memoir in 1925, General Bullard set the tone for future discussion of the combat performance and reliability of Negro troops in battle. He declared the Negro "hopelessly inferior, lazy, and slothful," and added:

> If you need combat soldiers, and especially if you need them in a hurry, don't put your time upon Negroes. The task of making soldiers of them and fighting with them, especially if there are any white people near, will be swamped in the race question. If racial uplift or racial equality is your purpose, that is another matter.[1]

Following the publication of Bullard's book, a number of studies concentrating on black combat performance in military conflicts, particularly during World War I, were undertaken by officers at the Army War College. These studies unanimously concluded that blacks were better suited for non-combat duties. Together with a plethora of disparaging remarks made at numerous informal gatherings, they would anneal white opinion about black soldiers and their unsuitability for combat for years to come. And it was this prevailing attitude of white commanders and white America that would provide the overarching context for military policy toward blacks during the inter-war years and in World War II, a policy of strict racial segregation combined with an implacably negative attitude toward black combatants.

It was against this historical background with the sword of Damocles hanging over their heads and reminding them of their past combat performance, that the men of the new 92nd Infantry Division entered combat during World War II in the Mediterranean Theater of Operations.

The history of the Italian Campaign, as it came to be called during World War II, is the history of an experiment. That experiment was born in the expediency of domestic politics and shaped in the crucible of war. The recommendation to commit large black units to combat in World War II came about by increments. White policy makers in the War Department, guided by its policy of not deploying blacks as combatants, were gradually experiencing a change of posture as black agitation mounted. By 1943, with United States military units engaged in offensive operations in the Pacific and in North Africa, black leaders added a new demand to their long list of grievances: the use of black units in combat. They argued, *inter alia*, that the ability to take up arms and fight should not be based on the color of one's skin, but on training, leadership, and motivation. If properly trained and motivated, blacks could fight for their country just as effectively as whites. Moreover, they argued, the time had come for blacks to demonstrate their patriotism and, if need be, to die for their country.

White leadership finally relented and allowed blacks to serve as combatants. The final recommendation came from the War Department's Advisory Committee on Negro Troop Policies and was crafted by Truman Gibson, the black civilian aide to the secretary of war. Secretary Henry Stimson was impressed by Gibson's ability and legal skills and trusted him for "his honesty and courage."[2] Gibson worked assiduously, drafting position papers on a number and variety of issues affecting blacks in the U.S. Army. His memoranda to Stimson and other senior War Department personnel were noted for their clarity, force of argument, and insight. They demonstrated his grasp of black issues, on which he painstakingly expatiated. In his capacity as civilian aide to the secretary of war, he also worked closely with assistant secretary of war John J. McCloy, who was Stimson's close adviser in the War Department and to whom all "colored matters" were referred. McCloy supported fully the Advisory Committee's recommendation on the grounds that it was far more cost effective and politically expedient to make ample use of black units, than to have them train endlessly in remote locations in the United States where they suffered discrimination and drew the attention of the black press.

Secretary Stimson and Army Chief of Staff General Marshall, while not completely amenable to the idea of deploying large black combat divisions to the war zone, were not opposed to the idea either. They reluctantly agreed to do so. In March 1944, the Army staff began to develop a series of detailed plans to deploy advance units of both the 92nd and 93rd infantry divisions to Italy and the Pacific respectively. Even at this late juncture, senior white policy makers in the War Department treated the whole affair as an experiment—a fact that Truman Gibson confirmed fifty years later in an interview at his home in Chicago. When asked to explain the ubiquitous charges of "mediocre and sluggish" combat performance by the 92nd Division, which he visited in Italy, Gibson unhesitatingly answered, "the division was programmed to fail from the inception."[3] The top leadership of the division saw itself as reporting the results of a military and social experiment.

At the end of the war, the division's commander, General Edward (Ned) Almond, confirmed in a Board of Review document that "the constant objective of top commanders of the 92nd Division has been to collect, evaluate, and draw conclusion[s] from reliable first-hand and at-the-time data which could be relied upon by the War Department in future employment of Negro military manpower."[4] And to determine how well black units would perform in combat, the Advisory Committee decided to commit one regimental combat team of the 93rd Division, already stationed in the Solomon Islands, to combat without special training and preparation. At Fort Huachuca, Arizona, a hand-picked regimental combat team, the 370th, selected from all units of the 92nd Division, was made ready for combat and subsequent deployment to the war zone in Italy.

The experience of black soldiers fighting in Italy may have been only an experiment to the War Department, but it produced an unexpected and (for many years) unacknowledged result: the molding and maturing of a diverse military command, the United States 92nd Infantry Division and its augmentation units. Within this process of maturation are many stories. There is the story of combat leadership and group accomplishment under adverse conditions in the rugged terrain of northern Italy. There is a human interest story of drama and excitement, of singularly heterogeneous elements drawn from all parts of the United States and brought together to meet the severe test of war. There are stories of individual bravery and courage under enemy fire. And there is the story of black soldiers fighting a war under senior white commanders, and under a cloud of distrust and opprobrium.

From the standpoint of time, the division's combat action in Italy was brief — slightly less than eight months — but it added, nevertheless, an interesting chapter to the history of World War II. For in this Mediterranean Theater of Operations were assembled men of different races and creeds, whose united efforts not only helped to destroy the German Army in Italy, but also to hasten the ultimate victory of Allied forces in the European Theater. At the same time, regrettably, some white commanders would give vent to cherished beliefs — some latent and some long suppressed — that they held about black soldiers. These negative beliefs would later form a conceptual prism through which black combat performance would be evaluated. And when the final chapter of this military and social experiment was written even before the war ended, it was these beliefs that would prejudice analysis and lead to faulty conclusions and highly inaccurate judgment about black soldiers.

The various elements of the 92nd Infantry Division entered into combat almost as soon as they arrived in Italy in the late summer and early fall of 1944. Many changes in the division's composition and organization, however, would occur before final victory in May 1945. For example, the entire division was completely reorganized before the final push toward the famed Italian city of Massa. This reorganization was not simply an exercise in manpower reshuffling and reassignment. Rather, it was metamorphic. It resulted in the creation of a non-black infantry division. Many chops and changes in organizational structure also took place soon after the division arrived on the peninsula. As a matter of record, there were organizational changes after every engagement with the enemy. The frequency of these changes and their attendant implications had a demoralizing effect on the troops and hurt their subsequent combat performance. But at the time, these changes were considered tactically necessary, and very little regard, if any, was given to their effect on unit cohesion and *esprit de corps*.

The geographic area in which the division fought covered more than 3,000 square miles of rugged territory stretching from Pontedera on the Arno River east of Pisa, thence west and north along the Ligurian coast to the old seaport of Genoa, made famous by Christopher Columbus. From there operations continued to Alessandria and westward as far as Turin, near the French border. Italy, still noted for its variegated landscape, was an extremely difficult terrain on which to conduct an offensive military operation. The Germans adroitly exploited their defensive advantages, making the Allies bleed for every mile of territory gained.

Although the division was part of the IV Corps, it spent nearly 40 percent of its combat time under the direct control of Headquarters, United States Fifth Army. Fifth Army and the British Eighth Army were the principal components of the 15th Army Group over which Lieutenant General Mark Clark assumed command in December 1944. Ten other divisions under the command of II and IV Corps also lined up with the 92nd Division in the American sector. On the eve of the Italian offensive, the reorganized and reinforced 92nd Infantry Division, under the command of Major General Edward Almond, held a front of twenty-three air-miles, its left flank on the Ligurian Sea southwest of the city of Massa. The line extended inland across a three-mile coastal plain, thence over a range of rugged mountains fifteen miles wide to the picturesque Serchio Valley. A panoramic view of the theater of operations revealed a seacoast on the western side, mountain mass in the middle, and an open valley at the eastern extension of the line.

The mission of the division was to stage an attack along the narrow coastal plain in order to divert the attention of the German high command from the main effort to be undertaken against them before the Po River Valley. Hence its objectives were limited yet important within the overall framework of operational strategy. Success for the division would augur well for the main attack of the Allied forces.

The attack of the 92nd, launched on April 5, 1945, more than served its purpose. All primary objectives were secured; the enemy facing the division's forces was badly battered and bruised, thereby forcing the commitment of all German reserves in the area. More significant, though, was the strategic reaction of the German high command. Gravely concerned with the threat imposed by the 92nd Division's thrust and momentum, it moved elements of the 90th Panzer Grenadier Division from the center of its securely held defensive line in an attempt to halt the 92nd's advance. This tactical move severely diminished the enemy's scanty strategic reserves at a time when the center of the German line was threatened with the Allied main effort in the Po Valley.

By April 22, 1945, the 92nd Division had seized all but the Aulla stronghold in its sector of the notoriously difficult and virtually impregnable Gothic Line. Then began the German withdrawal, a virtual rout, turning the once mighty and formidable Wehrmacht war machine into a disorganized rabble, fleeing in panic before Allied forces but unable to escape their complete surrender on May 2, 1945.

While the Ligurian Campaign ended in victory for the reorganized 92nd, the division's earlier lackluster combat performance and leadership were mired in controversy and fraught with numerous problems. The combat ability of black troops became highly suspect, giving rise to widespread assertions of incompetence and unreliability. But widespread, too, were the suspicions surrounding General Almond's leadership and strategic ability. The division's problems and initially poor combat performance, hence its failure, are traceable to many factors.

This book examines four big bones in the anatomy of the 92nd Infantry Division's failure. It will demonstrate that success on the battlefield and the fighting ability of troops are not predicated on the color of one's skin, but on training, motivation, morale, and leadership. In the 92nd Division's case, problems in these areas combined with tactical blunders on the battlefield were indeed a recipe for failure.

This book will also highlight the story of two of the division's heroes, examining their acts of bravery on the battlefield and noting the long, arduous struggle for proper recognition after the war came to an end in 1945. Second Lieutenant Vernon Baker and First Lieutenant John Fox would be finally recognized in January 1997 when President Bill Clinton presented them with the nation's highest honor for gallantry in combat, the Medal of Honor. Their heroism on the battlefield, long cherished by their comrades in the 92nd Infantry Division, was recounted in that presentation. Lieutenant Baker lived long enough, a life full of excitement and accomplishments, to stand before the president of the United States and have the nation's highest award for valor in combat placed around his neck. Then he returned home with his German wife to his isolated cottage in St. Maries, Idaho, to his old way of life. While receipt of the medal catapulted him into the limelight, he remained a private man who enjoyed the outdoors and hunting.

Lieutenant Fox, on the other hand, sacrificed his life in the Serchio Valley. That act of heroism went unrecognized for years before his widow, Mrs. Arlene Fox — who had lived long enough to witness this act of recognition of her husband's sacrifice and to tell the story of their love — finally received his posthumous award. Mrs. Fox is still a widow; she has never remarried. And every Christmas she remembers anew their short but wonderful life together.

The 92nd Infantry Division and General Edward Almond: Preparation for War

When General Edward Almond assumed command of the all-black 92nd Infantry Division in July 1942, World War II was already raging across the European continent, leaving a trail of unmitigated destruction and widespread devastation. Three months later when the division was activated at Fort McClellan, Alabama, American planes were streaming across the Atlantic and landing on British soil. By this time U.S. troops were already in Ireland, England, and Iceland. In a little over three weeks, Allied plans for the invasion of North Africa were on the verge of being operational. Russia demanded a second front while its troops halted the advance of the Nazis at Stalingrad. And when the British flanked Rommel's elite Africa Corps in the sands of the Egyptian desert at El Alamein, the German Luftwaffe continued to rain bombs on the busy streets of London. By 1942, the German war machine had rolled through the Balkans and across the rim of North Africa. Nazi victory seemed inevitable. But whatever notions of victory they entertained, and however grandiose their objective, the fate of the Nazi war machine was doomed to defeat when the United States entered the war.

In America, factories went into high gear rolling out tanks and munitions. A large work force was galvanized into action strengthening the "Arsenal of Democracy." The domestic atmosphere was charged with expectation and fear. And according to one military analyst, "Blackouts, air-raid wardens, civilian defense, censorship, draft boards, and ration books were all part of the American scene."[1] The massive utilization of human and material resources and the vast opportunities for technical innovation unleashed by this domestic state of affairs created a robust economy capable of sustaining a war on several fronts. But more importantly than the state of the economy was the fact that American leaders had the political will not only to commit this nation to war, but in doing so, to fight and win. They shared an understanding of what it would mean for the world, for America, and for democracy if Germany and its allies should prevail in this global conflict. Democracy and the rights of individual freedom, they inhered, must be defended at all cost. In short, Hitler's aggression and his diabolical ideology must be stopped, if not crushed.

Part of that commitment would inevitably involve the utilization of Negro manpower in this massive war effort. But the mobilization of blacks was on a completely segregated basis and primarily in non-combat units. Moreover, blacks were accepted into the armed forces in accordance with their proportion to the total population. This resulted in about 1.2 million blacks serving in World War II. And while the overwhelming majority of them served in support units and service roles, a small number, roughly 50,000, were engaged in actual combat against the enemy. This book is about one of those combat units, the 92nd Infantry Division that fought in Italy, and its commander. Although it was a black combat unit, all its senior officers were white, including its commander, Major General Edward Almond.

1. The 92nd Infantry Division and General Almond

Activation and Training

In an impressive ceremony on a clear, sunny day in October 1942, the 92nd Infantry Division was activated at Fort McClellan, Alabama. The governor-elect, the Honorable Chauncey Sparks, was on hand to give the welcoming address. Colonel Frank Barber, the division's chief of staff who was later killed in action in Italy in September 1944, read the activation address. And the newly appointed commander, Major General Edward "Ned" Almond, beaming with confidence and hopeful for the division, gave a remarkable speech in which he promised "fairness to every officer and man." Borrowing from Stonewall Jackson of Civil War fame, Almond said, "You may be whatever you resolve to be ... you are the 92nd Division. What you become depends on your resolution." To a round of thunderous applause he continued, "The 92d Division is primarily a combat division.... One of my principal aims is to produce a first class battlefield unit." Toward the accomplishment of that goal he bent his indefatigable energies, and while it remained with him throughout his command of the division, it never materialized to his satisfaction. Thus, his expectations on the one hand, and the division's poor combat performance on the other, combined with a pervasive climate of distrust, would eventually lead to the torrent of criticisms that would be hurled at the division.

On this, the division's official activation day, General Almond's enunciation revealed a latent course of action that would prove inimical to battlefield success. The production of "first class battlefield unit," he envisioned, would of necessity emphasize the mechanics of training and preparation. This overemphasis on the "mechanics of war," it would be shown, seriously undermined unit cohesion, and instead of promoting efficiency and efficacy among rank and file, it became their Achilles' heel. Almond's preoccupation with the mechanics of war rose to the point of obsession. In this state, he completely disregarded the human aspects of training and preparation. Little regard, if any, was given to ameliorating the immediate social conditions and thereby improving the morale of the men under his command. Blacks languished in a segregated environment and spent endless hours rehearsing drills and exercises to the point of exhaustion.

These routines resulted in the literal translation of Almond's promise to make these blacks a first class battlefield unit.

When the division's activation was finally consolidated on May 10, 1943, at Fort Huachuca in Arizona, a cadre of 128 officers and 1,200 enlisted men was transferred from the 93rd Infantry Division, also an all-black combat division, to join its ranks. Except for his division chief of staff and a few key staff officers, General Almond had no choice in the selection of these officers and enlisted men. Those who joined the 92nd Division later on were sent from the Army at large. Prior to consolidation at Fort Huachuca, General Almond and two of his general officer assistants had participated in a special four-day conference dealing with the activation and training of the division at Army Ground Forces in Washington from July 22 to July 26, 1942.

Following this conference, there was a series of special short courses attended by selected officers and enlisted men from the cadre. The objective was to bring about a more cohesive approach in the training and handling of black troops. It stemmed from the War Department's training philosophy that white commanders of Negro troops faced special problems in understanding blacks and their conditions in America. Not many white officers had handled or commanded black troops before. Thus the need to familiarize them with do's and don'ts, and to reinforce the War Department's policies regarding the command of Negro troops was important and deemed necessary. Moreover, the Department desired that black soldiers be used in the most effective manner. They were to be treated as Americans who happened to be black. And the accomplishment of this ideal involved "problems that are as technical as any other problem of personnel, and can be solved only with the benefit of special study, full information, a willingness to ask questions and try experiments, and a serious interest in finding adequate and reasonable solutions."[2] Sadly, these strategies to handle blacks and treat them as fellow Americans were never fully implemented by General Almond and several other senior white officers. Blacks were treated as second class citizens, fit only for menial tasks. This perception of them by the senior white leadership of the division eroded confidence and undermined unit cohesion.

Early in May 1943, troop trains carrying enlisted men and officers from Fort McClellan, Alabama; Camps Atterbury, Indiana; Breckin-

1. The 92nd Infantry Division and General Almond

ridge, Kentucky; and Robinson, Arkansas, began a westward journey to a desert location hundreds of miles away. Excitement and commotion filled the air as black soldiers and newly commissioned black officers hopped on board Pullman cars from their respective training installations. Since its activation months earlier, the division had never trained before as a single unit. Fort Huachuca would finally give them this opportunity to do so. It would also create a number of problems including distrust that would later prove disastrous. But little did anyone realize as they set out on this long ride that fourteen months later, they would embark on a similar journey, except this time it would be across the Atlantic Ocean.

The journey to Fort Huachuca took several days. But when the trains finally stopped and disgorged their human cargo of nearly 15,000 black soldiers, uncertainty and fear of isolation descended like a heavy cloud. The scene of gaiety and laughter that had filled the trains days before quickly evaporated, giving way to feelings of somberness and abandonment. A geographically isolated training facility that earlier housed the 93rd Infantry Division, Fort Huachuca was an established pioneer post located about 100 miles southeast of Tucson. It was first established during the last half of the nineteenth century and served as an advance headquarters and supply base for military personnel and settlers in the region during the Indian Wars of the 1870s and 1880s. Its remoteness from civilization stood in sharp contrast to other training facilities, and it would serve the purpose cherished by whites— isolate black soldiers from white communities.

When the four black military regiments were created by act of Congress before the turn of the century, this post also served as the home for the men of one of those regiments, the 10th Cavalry, while they guarded the United States–Mexico border during World War I. By the beginning of World War II, the cantonment area underwent massive reconstruction in order to accommodate the large contingents of the 93rd and later the 92nd infantry divisions. Fort Huachuca was surrounded by rugged but colorful mountains. The varied terrain though generally flat also included mountains and semi-desert. The topography compares favorably with sections of the Apennines in Italy. It was an ideal military training facility — isolated, quiet, expansive, and lending itself well to close-in training. Moreover, the climate eliminates the "rainy-day schedule" so common to other military posts. It meant that training could be a continuous activity with little or no interruption.

Fort Huachuca was also the only "suitable" training facility that could adequately accommodate a unit as large as the 92nd Infantry Division. And the distance between towns and cities surrounding this facility and the social constraints imposed by a generally white society reinforced its attractiveness. The nearest town, Tombstone, was twenty-six miles away and deserted. Bisbee and Naco were forty-two miles away but inhospitable in their reception to Negro soldiers. Along the streets of Naco and other towns such as Nogales and Aqua Prieta located across the Mexican border south of Fort Huachuca, black soldiers could find adequate amusement centers. But stringent gas rationing imposed by the War Department made transportation unavailable for soldiers to visit these facilities. Nevertheless, many blacks took their chances and ventured into these towns.

However, a small community, Fry, just outside the main entrance of the fort, sprang up when civilian construction workers built it. Here ladies of the night plied their wares and spread venereal diseases like gonorrhea to hundreds of black troops. And here also prostitution, bootleg whiskey, and gambling abounded in dilapidated shacks and shanties that lacked running water and latrines. The area was enclosed in a barbed wire barricade complete with a military police and prophylactic station. One section of this little thriving community, known as "the Hook," was occupied on a regular basis by over a hundred prostitutes and swelled to another 200 on payday and weekends. One veteran who requested that he remain anonymous remembered that on every payday, soldiers would form long lines outside this little village just for half an hour of pleasure with prostitutes. And it was also at Fort Huachuca that the newly arrived all-black 92nd Infantry Division would consolidate their training and test their skills in marksmanship, navigation, military drills, and unit tactics for the next nine months before departing for the "Louisiana Maneuvers" in early February 1944. Here, they learned the mechanics of war and endured the ennui of repetition. Here also, they experienced some of the worst forms of racial discrimination. These experiences, difficult to overcome, would leave searing memories for many of these men.

All but five months of the division's training was accomplished at Fort Huachuca. For seventeen months, training at this location was directed toward creating, according to the division's commander, "a physically toughened, efficient battle force thoroughly skilled, and imbued with the desire to close with and destroy any enemy engaged."[3] The overall training followed War Department's and Army Ground Forces' prescribed programs. But in addition to routine drills, unit tactics, endurance marches, and small arms firing, the division commander instituted more combat exercises and a series of special training activities involving mountain operations, stream crossing, aggressive patrolling, and combined exercises using tanks and tank destroyers. Tests and inspections were regular aspects of training. When these revealed deficiencies, additional training was prescribed. For example, unit and combined training exercises were increased from twenty to twenty-eight weeks, and rifle marksmanship took longer and required three to four times more ammunition for instructional practice than in the average white units.

While Army plans called for a newly activated division to be trained and ready for combat between ten to twelve months after activation, the 92nd Division training period lasted well over nineteen months. When asked to explain this anomaly after the war, General Almond, in an interview in 1975, made the point that they "took longer than the average division for the training period prior to entry into combat because it took longer for the instructor to secure a sink-in result in any instruction that we offered."[4]

The division's overall training program was dictated and at the same time constrained by two major factors. First was the excessively high level of illiteracy among enlisted men. A former chief of staff of the division made the succinct point that at "one time we had to stop training and spend eight weeks teaching the men to read … we found they couldn't read the field manuals." This officer went on to say that while "some of them were dammed good Infantrymen, [many] couldn't read a compass or a map or a field manual."[5] The problem of widespread illiteracy (well over 60 percent) was generally recognized. It placed an unusually heavy burden on training officers and led to an extension of training time. To reduce what was commonly accepted in everyday human interaction "as understandable language to an even lower level was not easy to do without subconsciously berating one's listeners for that lack of 'intelligence' which required annoying additional effort on the part of the instructor."[6]

The illiteracy problem was further compounded by Army's policy that stated that black troops, regardless of their level of educational attainment, were to be attached to and trained in the same unit. Army General Comprehensive Test (AGCT) ratings for the 92nd Division showed a whopping 71.3 percent in categories IV and V, the lowest in the rating scale. When compared to the average figure of 45.4 percent in other combat divisions, that percentage for the 92nd seemed extremely large. This finding ought to have alerted Army personnel that these men should not have been allowed to join the military, or should not have been bundled together and placed in the same outfit. The idea to lump large numbers of illiterate recruits in the same unit was ill conceived, and the practice to continue in this mode of operation in spite of persistent problems was time-wasting and highly uneconomical. Nevertheless, Army policy prevailed, but at a considerable cost. Interestingly, the Army did not bunch up all its white recruits who scored at levels IV and V in the same unit. They were widely dispersed, and the overall results were spectacular. Had the same tactic been employed for blacks also, the results would have been more encouraging.

Second, the recalcitrant, twin-axed problem of low morale and malingering also had a devastating effect on training, effectiveness, and efficiency. Concerns with the importance of high morale in training and on the battlefield were given considerable attention by the War Department. Formidable obstacles stood in the way of the black enlisted man. Ulysses Lee, a black military historian, put it well when he said that "On a new and unfamiliar post, the first few days could be filled with disturbing questions for the Negro soldier who wished to avoid embarrassment and possibly serious entanglements with local rules and customs. Would he be served if he tried to make a purchase at the main post exchange, or was there a special branch exchange for Negro units?... To many Negro soldiers the uncertainty of their status was as damaging to morale as the knowledge of definite restrictions."[7]

Also contributing to low morale were the ubiquitous signs of "white only" at many training posts. At Fort Huachuca, for example, duplicate facilities were the rule: two hospitals, one for whites and one for blacks; two sets of civilian living quarters; two officers' clubs; two sets of dining areas; the list goes on. Black soldiers felt that they were being constantly reminded of their inferior status and second class citizenship. Reminiscing on the time spent in training at Fort Huachuca, Lieutenant Vernon Baker, a black junior officer and platoon leader, said that black officers could not enter the commander's office through the front entrance. They had to use the rear of the building instead.

Reacting to concerns of low morale among black troops in the 92nd Infantry Division, General Benjamin Davis, the first black to be promoted to the rank of brigadier general, noted evidence of this decline and the rising growth of dissatisfaction and resentment within the division as evidenced by stoning of officers riding through enlisted areas. He made the following remarks in his report to the inspector general after his summer visit to Fort Huachuca in 1943:

> General Almond has, in the opinion of the inspector general, overlooked the human element in the training of this Division. Great stress has been placed upon the mechanical perfection in the execution of training missions. Apparently not enough consideration has been given to the maintenance of a racial understanding between white and colored officers and men. The execution of ceremonies with smartness and precision, and the perfunctory performance of military duties is taken as an indication of high morale. This is not true with the colored soldier. He can be driven to perform without necessarily having a high morale.[8]

Malingering and its attendant manifestation of straggling, another major constraint to recruit training, seemed to have been well mastered by hundreds of black soldiers at Fort Huachuca. Repeatedly, men would feign sickness and lengthen the line to the medical center every morning. At one point it became very comical to listen to soldiers complaining of pain in every conceivable part of their anatomy. It was a serious epidemic. In most cases the doctors could find nothing that was physically wrong with these men. Almost every day of training, ten to fifteen men in each company would claim sickness or complain of pains that could not be diagnosed or ascertained with any degree of certainty by the post's doctor. In a twenty-five-mile prescribed march, recalled Almond, more than 2,000 men were taken out of several units and treated for a variety of illnesses in spite of having successfully completed the journey. Large numbers feigned physical ailments of a disqualifying nature. "The problem," according to the commander, "developed suddenly and grew rapidly to large proportions. It was curbed somewhat by prompt disciplinary action."[9] Nevertheless, malingering persisted, and when the division was ordered overseas, there were nearly a thousand men — pronounced malingerers — who were in the "Casual Camp" at Fort Huachuca. These "casuals" or unfits would subsequently be taken overseas and committed to the combat zone.

As training progressed from the lower structural levels of platoons to companies, to battalions, and regiments, the division was finally able to carry out its D (for division) series of tactical exercises in December 1943. Four months later, it participated in the Louisiana Maneuvers from February to April 1944. Although its overall performance in these exercises was not spectacular, it was not lackluster either. Nevertheless, the division received a satisfactory rating, and was finally given the nod for overseas deployment.

Segregation and Turbulence

Established largely by rumors and reinforced by the Army general staff's conviction that black troops had cut and run, and had failed to perform aggressively in combat during World War I, segregation survived to permeate every facet of the Army during World War II. The experience with black troops during World War I in Europe cast a dark shadow over the formation of the Army's racial policy in World War II. Entrenched deeply in the War Department for over five decades, segregation of troops on the basis of race was the Army's official policy during this global conflict. But the Army was not alone in its practice of segregation. It merely reflected the dominant societal culture of the time.

Insidious as it may be viewed today, segregation on the eve of World War II was the law of the land. It was a fundamental problem before the War Department, and despite changes sanctioned by the Selective Service Act of 1940, the basic policies of the Army regarding blacks remained essentially unchanged during the war. In large sections of the country where lynching and beatings were everyday occurrences and where Jim Crow laws dominated, "White supremacy had existed as a literal fact of life and death."[10] Few stopped to consider that the key factor in efficient combat performance was not predicated on the race of the fighting troops, but the fact that they were segregated; that segregation was not the remedy but the cause of the frailty and poor performance that beset many black units.

While it was true that segregation adversely affected the training and subsequent combat performance of the 92nd Division, it must also be noted that a number of other factors, some intangible and some closely related to segregation, also contributed to the problems facing the division. The late Hondon Hargrove, a former black officer with the 92nd Division and author of a well-researched and balanced appraisal of the Buffalo Soldiers in Italy, put his finger on the pulse of the problem when he asserted that there was "in constant ferment — an intangible, elusive undercurrent of resentment, bitterness, even despair and hopelessness among black officers and enlisted men in the division."[11] Perceived by blacks as the root cause of most, if not all, of their problems, segregation did indeed exert a devastating effect on training, morale, and performance, and it undermined every other aspect of cohesion and leadership within the division. But segregation, though baneful and incorrigible, was not totally responsible for all the festering and recalcitrant problems the division experienced. The issues of leadership, mutual distrust between blacks and whites, and a sense of a lack of identification were also responsible.

A major barrier to the development of leadership in the 92nd Division stemmed from the employment of black and white officers under conditions that emphasized differences in officers' ethnic origins, rather than similarities in their goals and responsibilities. White America at the time was notorious for its obsession with ethnicity and Euro-centric superiority, and this orientation was clearly manifested in Army policies. The differences in management and utilization of black and white officers were based on Army Ground Forces policy established in late 1942. This policy clearly advocated that no black officer was to outrank or command any white officer in the same unit. Its effect was devastating for the black officer because it confirmed a different status for him within the division. Moreover, it resulted in a command structure in which black officers provided the vast majority of second and first lieutenants, and a parsimonious number of captains. All senior commanders had to be and were white. In the 92nd Division, there were only six black field grade officers in the combat arms, and all of them were in the field artillery battalions. Two were lieutenant colonels and commanded the 597th and 600th battalions; four were majors. Two of these majors served as executive officers and the other two served as operations officers (S-3) for the 597th and 600th.

This policy also countenanced and gave sanction to the idea that no black officer, no matter his level of competency and education, or even his military training and experience, could perform assigned duties better than any white officer, no matter how incompetent the latter might be. It also sent a clear signal to the enlisted men in the division that their black commissioned leaders were not "full-fledged" officers or as knowledgeable and competent as white officers. This perception created leadership problems at the platoon level where the need for trust and confidence in commissioned leadership was most salient. The net result generated by this policy was the creation of invidious and intractable distinctions, perceived or real, between officers in the same units. Thus, most black officers within the division resented the social matrix that confined them to subordinate positions. Many felt that the development of ingenuity and the assumption of responsibility would not be awarded by advancement to positions of greater responsibility within the organization. And not a few embraced the notion that they were uniformed symbols, doomed to receive at best a grudging acceptance as officers from their white superiors and counterparts, and uncertain and questioning recognition as leaders from their subordinates.

Mutual suspicions, distrust, and dislike between blacks and whites were not new phenomena in American society. Within the 92nd Division, these attitudes were very pervasive and terribly destructive of morale and cohesion. Hargrove confirmed this when he noted that "There was a feeling of mutual dislike and distrust between black and white officers. Many of them — black as well as white — did not want to serve in the division because of this. Many white officers did not *like* black soldiers, and many submitted requests for transfers right up to the time of embarkation. General Almond's policy was to approve such requests whenever possible."[12]

Racial tension, exacerbated by feelings of distrust, flared up in the division during both training and combat. The former civilian aide to the secretary of war, Truman Gibson, recalled witnessing the troops booing General Almond on an inspection visit to Fort Huachuca.[13] A former Maryland congressman, Parren Mitchell, who served as a company commander in the 370th Infantry Regiment, remembered initially being refused service at the white officer's mess on the day in 1943 that he reported to the division.[14] During training, many blacks struck back, occasionally with violence. Enlisted men stoned a car occupied by white officers, and a white lieutenant was hit in the head with a shovel while asleep in his tent.[15] However, not all black soldiers resorted to these measures. Many resisted passively, preferring a safer approach rather than outright confrontation. So by the time the division was ready for overseas deployment in the summer of 1944, over two thousand of its soldiers, men who were physically fit but deemed psychologically unfit for combat, were in the division's "Casual Camp."[16]

Distrust and racial incidents were also carried over to the combat zone. Shortly after the division arrived in Italy, a white officer in the 317th Engineer Combat Battalion was shot in the foot while he was asleep in his tent. The investigating officer, a captain from the division's Inspector General Section, was unable to discover the assailant's identity, but clearly and forthrightly described the battalion's dismal state of morale: "The EM [enlisted men] dislike their officers; the officers dislike each other; and they all seemingly dislike their Bn [battalion] Commander." The captain's report also made clear that perceptions of racial discrimination were an important, though not the only, factor contributing to the explosive situation in the battalion. He recommended that the 317th's commander, Lieutenant Colonel Edward Rowney, be relieved, but General Almond declined to act on this recommendation.[17]

Distrust, fueled by racial animosities and dislike, also touched a black officer assigned to the division's General Staff. In February 1945, two months before the Spring Offensive, Captain Leroy Clay, a Negro officer assigned to the G-3 (Operations) Section was convicted by court-martial for disobeying a direct order. Lieutenant Bert Cumby, a black officer assigned to the Adjutant General Section, refused to testify on Clay's behalf at the court-martial hearings. He subsequently received a letter threatening his life:

> You should be ashamed of yourself.... We know that if any Negro Officer in the 92nd Division, knows the inner workings of the division's vicious circle, you do. We know that you have been exposed to more trickery in the 92nd Division than any other Negro Officer in the division.... The 92nd Division has a worldwide reputation for its injustices to the Negro Officer and enlisted man. It was that way in the United States ... and it will continue to be a slave unit for white masters as long as weak and indifferent Negro officers like yourself, continue to watch justice raped, and say, "I don't know the facts in the case." ... We have just begun to fight, not for a bunch of incompetents who dictate life and death to us in the lily-white 92nd Division, but for ourselves. We know now too well, who our enemies are, and they are not only Germans. Our enemy is that race-hating white man, the kind and type the Army has selected to "command" the "Negro Division," and the 92nd Division. You will never be able to stand between our cause and justice again. Over here life is cheap, very cheap. The cheapness of you, as an officer makes your own life, in our sight, cheaper.[18]

Signed only with a cross, the letter is important not only for its contents and description of racial prejudice and distrust perceived within the division by black soldiers, but also because it reveals a high level of suspicion and hatred enough to divide black soldiers from each other.

Compounding the problems generated by racism and distrust was the overall "aloofness attitude" displayed by the division's senior white commanders. Many observers noted that the division's leadership seemed unaware of the damage racial conflict and antagonism was doing. Following a visit to the division in the summer of 1943 at Fort Huachuca, Brigadier General Benjamin O. Davis reported to the War

Department that it was very apparent that General Almond had not given "enough consideration ... to the maintenance of a racial understanding between white and colored officers and men."[19] Truman Gibson, in his March 1945 report suggested, with respect to the accounts of undisciplined withdrawals by black infantrymen under fire, that "The underlying reasons are quite generally unknown in the division."[20] And when complaints of negative racial attitudes and practices were made and brought to the attention of General Almond, "He seldom took action with his battalion or regimental commanders or members of his Headquarters Staff against whom these complaints were made." Hargrove also noted Almond's indifference to complaints ventilated by blacks, and his recalcitrance to change or alter a contentious and highly unrealistic policy: "No black officers commanding companies, battalions or regiments and no black staff officers at battalion level or above."[21]

The virtual absence of a sense of identification was another problem that seriously affected cohesion and effectiveness. This problem could be traced to the formative months of the division when different elements underwent training at vastly different locations. Activation found the division headquarters and special troops at Fort McClellan, Alabama, several hundred miles away from the regimental combat teams. Reminiscing on this period, Hargrove noted that "[A] sense of identification with battalion and regiment and with the division as a whole, was never quite completely achieved.... During the early months, officers and enlisted men never had an opportunity to see the officers and enlisted men in the other combat teams; and so, different procedures and atmospheres, influenced by the personalities and racial attitudes of the commanders and staffs, as well as the oppressive racial climate in the four widely separated training areas, led to differences in methods of resolving problems."[22] This widespread dispersion during the formative period of the division hampered division-wide development of *esprit*. Different procedures and different atmospheres developed in each of the four enclaves and had a negative effect on morale. Moreover, the personalities of senior white commanders and the racial climate of the individual geographic region combined to exert a serious effect on the development of unit cohesion and a sense of camaraderie.

Thus, when the division was consolidated at Fort Huachuca, there was an escalation of dormant antipathies which, when the division was scattered, were less intense. In short, consolidation reinforced and brought into sharper focus a sense of alienation and many other nascent and festering problems. The commanding general repeatedly demonstrated a lack of sensitivity toward the myriad intangible problems, most if not all traceable to racial segregation, facing the division. Had he been able to understand the special needs and sensibilities of black troops, and was willing to deal with the rigidities and strictures imposed by social segregation, it was quite possible that the 92nd Infantry Division would have been a very different fighting force. Thus, the question of leadership and the role of General Almond are extremely important to our understanding of the history of the Black Buffaloes, and to this we now turn.

The Commander

He was vilified and castigated and yet at the same time held in high esteem by many of his white colleagues. But among black enlisted men and officers, he was branded a racist and perceived a poor military strategist. No senior white commander in World War II stirred up more controversy among his men and at the same time invoked such levels of animosity and bittersweet feelings than Major General Edward Almond, commander of the 92nd Infantry Division. He was neither an enigmatic figure nor a well-liked military leader. Yet to many he appeared distant, detached, and aloof. What kind of a man and leader was General Almond? Are all the invectives and castigation hurled at him absolutely true? Was he indeed a racist, someone who disliked and thought less of blacks, and was he that knowledgeable about blacks and black culture as he claimed to be? And to what extent was his leadership of the division responsible for its failure and poor combat performance? These and other questions we shall attempt to explore in the remaining pages of this chapter.

Born in Luray, Virginia, on the 12th of December 1892, Edward Almond was the eldest of three children. He grew up, according to him, in a happy family, surrounded by loving and caring parents who were fairly comfortable. He described his mother as "a wonderful woman, friendly with all types of people and all her neighbors and was very popular."[23] His father was a salesman of heavy farm machinery who called upon his numerous clients by horse and buggy throughout Page and Culpeper counties of rural Virginia. When he was ten, the family moved to Culpeper County where he attended Culpeper High School. Compared with Luray, Culpeper was more developed and progressive—a town of about 3,000 people, with several lawyers, ministers, and merchants—many of whom had an influence on the young and impressionable Almond.

During his high school days in Culpeper, Almond became a member of a National Guard company, attending two summer camps with other members. He was greatly influenced by the Commonwealth's attorney, Edwin Gibson, who was also a captain of the Culpeper Minutemen, a National Guard unit that attained a reputation during the Civil War. According to Almond, "The unit had retained its interest in military activities so that children of the Civil War soldiers became members of the National Guard company."[24] While a member and later a sergeant in Company B, Almond developed an interest in the military and aspired to attend the United States Military Academy at West Point. He was an above average student during his high school days, excelling in history, English, and mathematics in that order.

While the Civil War settled once and for all the questions of territorial unification and slavery in America, it left in its path, at the same time, a trail of destruction, grief, and socioeconomic upheavals. Many of the older folks in Culpeper who survived this carnage knew family and friends who had been killed in the war. And "One of the ways they expressed it was their memorial day services [held] once a year in which all the people with any responsibility would go to the cemetery and put flowers on the graves of the Civil War dead and discuss the terrors and the hardships imposed by [this event] which had occurred only 30 or 40 years before."[25] The young Almond remembered these annual gatherings and recalled very vividly the bitterness and resentfulness expressed by many in Culpeper that the Civil War had caused. No doubt he was affected by these sentiments and years later when he was asked about his own feelings toward Northerners, he replied, "We always called anybody from the north of the Mason-Dixon Line a Yankee and looked at them askance, especially if we didn't know them well."[26]

Developing an interest in history at an early age, Almond was also fascinated by the military exploits of Napoleon and Bismarck. The Battle of Marengo, fought in the Po Valley in Italy, was particularly interesting to him, and little did he realize then that thirty years later, this very geographic area would fall in his sector of military operations during World War II. During the spring term of his senior year in high school, he was seized by an attack of appendicitis and rushed to hospital in Charlottesville from his home in Culpeper. After four different operations during a ten-day period, the worst was over. Unable to continue attending school for a short period, the young Almond was allowed to graduate with a diploma suspended. It was not until he entered the Virginia Military Academy (VMI) in 1912 that he finally received his high school diploma.

Financially strapped and unable to attend a private college, Almond turned to the military. From an early age he had expressed an interest in attending West Point and becoming an officer in the United States Army. But when Claude Swanson, a senator from Virginia and a friend of Almond's father who had promised the young man an appointment to West Point after high school, died suddenly in 1911, all hopes of a military career seemed dashed. And just when he cogitated the wider implications of not being able to attend West Point, his mother came to his rescue. She knew a Virginia state senator, George Browning, who when he learned of Almond's interest in the military, suggested that he go to VMI instead, and offered him a state cadetship that carried with it considerable financial assistance. The young aspirant to a military career was elated and very grateful to this benefactor.

At VMI Almond quickly learned about the traditions of this great and illustrious military institution, and adopted himself quite well to a rigid and disciplined life style. No doubt the imposing statue of Stonewall Jackson, strategically placed on the edge of the parade ground, inspired every recruit as his company marched past it day after day. Entering VMI three months after his surgical operation for appendicitis, Almond was spared the hardships of being a "rat" during his first year. The institute doctor saw the severity of his condition and had him excused from strenuous training and from the "hazing" that first year students or "rats" were routinely subjected to. During his four years at VMI, Almond met and cultivated a lasting friendship with many of his colleagues and alumni. VMI had developed an outstanding reputation for producing good officers and many of these young men were given the opportunity to serve in the U.S. military right after graduation. General Pershing frequently referred to VMI as the West Point of the South, and it was also the place where General George Marshall, who later became Army chief of staff, graduated from. When asked if he regretted going to VMI, Almond curtly replied, "No," and added, "Once I became a graduate of VMI I have always been inspired by its principles and never regretted my attendance there compared to any other school, including West Point. I admire West Point tremendously, but I still appreciate the accomplishments of VMI's civilian school which does a fine job in preparing individuals for military service."[27]

Soon after his graduation from VMI, the young Almond joined the U.S. Army as a junior officer. He rose to the rank of captain very quickly and then attended the Army Staff College at Fort Leavenworth. In early 1933 he and his young family along with close friends undertook a tour of China, visiting the Great Wall, the last ten miles of which was completed on donkeys. The small group also visited Japan, Mongolia, and the Philippines. Returning to San Francisco in mid–1933, Almond journeyed by train across the United States to Washington, D.C., in time to attend the Army War College, which was at the time located at Fort McNair. The War College is a military institution designed for senior officers. Here discussion and training centered on the wars of the past, and on political or governmental control of states. The course of study represented for these officers an advance in intellectual pursuit of national events rather than with the operation of troops.

Soon after the completion of his year's course at the War College, Almond was assigned to the General Staff of the Army in the Latin American section of the military intelligence division of the War Department General Staff in Washington, D.C. Considering it an honor and being somewhat unprepared for intelligence work, Almond commented that his selection "had been made by people who had known

[him] in the years before, not only for what [he had] accomplished at the War College but for the general tone of [his] service."[28] The chief of the Intelligence Branch, which was known at the time as G-2, was a friend of both Almond and General George Marshall, a graduate of VMI and Army chief of staff. Almond was assigned to the Latin American section although he neither read nor wrote Spanish. This section comprised the central and southern republics, twenty countries in all, very diverse in size, ethnic composition, level of economic and political development, and type of government. He was assigned to all these countries, except Mexico.

An assignment to the Army Intelligence Branch was not considered prestigious — it ranked below the estimate of the Army in general (G-3 and G-4). In short, intelligence work was not an automatic leader toward a command. Almond was disappointed. He preferred an assignment to the G-3 section, which would have given him the experience needed to command a regiment or a division. But he accepted his new assignment with a determination to do his best and not disappoint his superiors. His work was to prepare the records of the reports that were submitted to him by military attachés operating from the American Embassy in these countries. These reports were divided into five sections, namely geographic, economic, political, military, and social. Almond's major task was to update these records and prepare an annual intelligence assessment report on all nineteen countries assigned to him. It was tedious work, but he enjoyed it, learning a lot about these countries. It was also at this time while he was assigned to Latin America that the Monroe Doctrine was initiated. Almond and his colleagues at G-2 felt that the Latin American countries thoroughly accepted the Monroe Doctrine and would join the United States in opposing an incursion by a foreign country (mainly a European state) of their territory. However, many saw this foreign policy posture as another attempt by the U.S. government to exercise its hegemony over the entire region.

After spending four years in G-2 doing intelligence work, Almond set off for the Air Corps Tactical School at Maxwell Field in Montgomery, Alabama, in 1938. This was his first choice of assignment that was readily granted to him. Still hopeful that someday he would be given a G-3 command assignment, Almond believed that attending the Air Corps Tactical school (now the Air War College) would give him, a ground officer, a better understanding of the capabilities and possibilities of the Air Force in support of ground operations. The course was attended mainly by pilots and built around three aspects of air operation — observation, attack, and bombardment. Almond was particularly interested in air support of ground operations. He felt that the Air Corps had been until this time more concerned with strategic air bombings, and bombing and fighter pilot operations, than it had been in support of ground troops, especially close-in support. Although he ventilated his concerns in classes and in private conversations with pilots and instructors, he still felt, after completing his year at Maxwell, that the Air Corps was concentrating too much on their own favorite tactics and not on a coordinated effort to support ground troops.

From Maxwell he went straight to the Naval War College at Newport, Rhode Island, as a student, an unheard of situation. How was it that he was able to receive a second year of schooling in a different service school? In his own words Almond confessed: "I requested and sought every means I could with the people I knew on the general staff."[29] When Almond was finally granted permission to attend the Naval War College, he became the first officer in the history of the United States military to attend all three service schools. It was an unusual accomplishment. He discovered a similarity in orientation between the Army and the Naval war colleges. Both institutions concentrated on improving the intelligence and understanding of their officers in strategic operations and political issues of government and international politics. The course at the Naval War College, however, was centered around the strategic operations of Naval forces and Naval engagements rather than amphibious operations. Almond found the year at Rhode Island to be extremely profitable, gaining many acquaintances and cultivating new and important friendships with individuals such as Admiral Hall, who later became the assistant amphibious commander of the force that took General Patton across the Atlantic to North Africa, and Admiral Halsey, a fleet commander in the Pacific Command under Admiral Nimitz.

After completing his program at the Naval War College, Almond returned to his old post for another five months in the Latin American section of G-2 Division of the General Staff in June 1940. During this short stint, he made periodic reports to General Miles, chief of G-2, about the dissatisfaction of the general Mexican population and the strong possibility of a popular uprising. When the latter did not come to pass, an indication of assessment failure on his part, Almond felt that the time had come for a troop duty assignment. Intelligence appraisal was not his forte and he felt quite silly after his recent prediction failed to materialize. Again, he relied on contacts and friendships. This time Colonel Charles Ryder, a former colleague who was in charge of the China desk at G-2, and now the chief of staff of the newly formed VI Corps, contacted Almond just before Christmas in 1940 and offered him the job of G-3. Colonel Ryder was a very capable military officer. He was a graduate of West Point (class of 1915) and a close friend and classmate of General Eisenhower. He and Almond were "great friends and associates" at Fort Benning, at Leavenworth, and at G-2 on the War Department General Staff. So when the call came, Almond seized the opportunity and in January 1941 moved to Providence, Rhode Island, where he became G-3 of VI Corps. Almond always wanted troop duty assignment and the exercise of leadership but was denied this for eight years—five in G-2 and three in staff colleges—none of which prepared him for a senior leadership position in military operations in wartime, not to mention the command of black troops.

The VI Corps was a newly formed military organization with two principal units, the 1st Division stationed at Fort Devens, and the 26th Division in the Boston area, which was National Guard. Almond's job was a demanding one, unsuited for someone who had had no recent exposure to military operations, inspections, and training. As a newly formed unit, VI Corps was woefully weak in basic infantry training and in small field operations. Yet he was given the task to develop training schedules, inspect units that composed VI Corps, and design maneuvers that would test troops' capabilities on the battlefield. The Corps conducted maneuvers in the field in August 1941 after undergoing a period of extensive training that focused on technical improvements. Participating in this field exercise with the VI Corps was the 101st Cavalry Regiment, a Negro unit from New York. Three months later in November, the Corps moved by truck to participate in the

Carolina maneuvers. Before the exercises began, Almond was promoted to the rank of full colonel in October. It was at the end of these exercises when the Corps was heading back to their headquarters in Rhode Island that Japan attacked Pearl Harbor, and catapulted the United States into World War II.

January 1942 found America preparing for war against Japan. The country was in turmoil and in a bellicose mood. Revenge gripped the nation. With the escalation of military activities came a greater demand for trained leadership. Colonel Charles Ryder was promoted to brigadier general and transferred to the 90th Division just after the bombing of Pearl Harbor, leaving the chief of staff position in VI Corps vacant. So in January 1942, Colonel Almond, who had spent exactly one year with the VI Corps as G-3, was appointed chief of staff. However, he still coveted a leadership position in troop assignment. In his own words thirty-three years later he opined: "Even though I was appointed Chief of Staff of the VI Corps, my desire was still…assignment with troops with the hope that I would get to be a battlefield leader and be transferred to wherever the war was being fought."[30] Little by little Almond's dream of becoming a military commander on the battlefield was turning into reality. No sooner was he made chief of staff of VI Corps in January 1942 than he was promoted to brigadier general three months later and then transferred to the 93rd Infantry Division as assistant division commander.

Such a meteoric rise in rank and position was not based entirely on brilliance or adept military capabilities. Almond was neither. He knew, however, the right people and he was well connected in the Army's military hierarchy. Two of his friends, General Mark Clark, chief of staff to General McNair, and Lloyd Brown, G-3 of the Army's ground force staff, were instrumental in gaining him promotion and at the same time securing him his new position with the 93rd Infantry Division that was undergoing training at Fort Huachuca. Almond believed that these two gentlemen had observed his "planning and conduct" of the Carolina exercises and were impressed with his capabilities, thus they recommended him for promotion. Before taking up his new assignment with the 93rd, Almond underwent three weeks of advanced training in general officers' duty and troop development at Fort Benning, Georgia. He spent exactly five months as assistant division commander of the all-black 93rd Infantry Division, during which time he concentrated on the development of the three regiments in operational tactics and sorting out myriad administrative problems that included minor court cases, inspections, equipment, and re-supply. The division was already undergoing training at Fort Huachuca when Almond arrived. Activated the previous fall and engaged in small unit training, it was attempting to consolidate its disparate elements into a division when Almond took up his new position. But his tenure was short-lived. After five months, he was transferred again.

His meteoric rise continued. In September 1942, Almond was made commander of the newly activated 92nd Infantry Division. Once again his right connections paid off. He was recommended to General Marshall, who knew him well, by his friend Lloyd Brown, G-3 of the Army ground forces. Many observers charged that Almond, like other commanders of black troops before him, was selected to command the 92nd Division because he was a Southerner. His selection for both assignments, first with the 93rd and second with the 92nd, chimed with the War Department's posture that Southern white officers possessed better leadership qualifications and therefore are more suitable than their Northern counterparts to command and lead black troops. Almond endorsed this belief when he explained that General Marshall felt comfortable with the idea that Southern whites "understood the characteristic of the Negro and his habits and inclinations."[31] Whatever modicum of truth resided in this outlandish yet real idea, Almond felt that since he was from Virginia, he had an understanding of Southern customs, Negro capabilities, and the attitudes of Negroes. In short, his Southern upbringing endowed him with the right credentials to understand and manage black troops. Nothing could be further from the truth.

As a young man growing up in Luray and Culpeper County, Virginia, Almond never once interacted with blacks. Such was also the case during his four years at VMI. That Almond understood the characteristics of Negroes and was familiar with their capabilities and inclinations was indeed a palpable stretch of anyone's imagination. From a field perspective, Almond had no experience as a division commander and only a short stint in troop assignment duties. He had spent only three of his twenty-four years of service in troop-leading positions. His choice, it would appear, was based more on his connections and somewhat less in his ability as a tough trainer. The former chief of staff of the 92nd during World War II affirmed that Almond was "the apple of George Marshall's eye," and that he was "selected by Marshall because he thought Ned was the best trainer he had, no question about it."[32] Marshall was also persuaded by the idea that southern whites knew how to command black troops.

Like thousands of whites during his time, Almond could not have escaped the influence of the dominance of race issues and racial manifestations in American society. Blacks, still not free in America, were considered genetically inferior and treated little better than slaves. And as a commander of a black division, he could not imagine anything other than a segregated unit. His command was notorious for segregating officers and facilities. He was highly insensitive to the impact of such strict social segregation on the sensibilities of black officers, and the effects such negative treatment would have on their motivation to lead troops into battle. Moreover, he vehemently opposed integration of the Armed Forces to his dying day in 1975, believing that the Army had made a terrible mistake. It was an indisputable fact that he believed in the inferiority of the Negro race. Commenting in "The Utilization of Negro Manpower in the Army," a study prepared in 1959 by the Operations Research Office of Johns Hopkins University under contract with the Department of the Army, Almond asserted that "It is absurd to contend that with the characteristics demonstrated by Negroes in general, in the views of those who know them and had an opportunity to know them, to consider that such characteristics will not undermine and deteriorate the white army unit into which the Negro is integrated." And on the utilization of blacks for combat he commented: "[I]t is very questionable whether people of the traits exhibited by Negroes should be entrusted in key combat units in any degree."[33]

In spite of his racist beliefs and strict enforcement of segregation policies when he commanded the 92nd Infantry Division, Almond was unquestionably a technocrat of a commander. He was incredibly organized, made detailed and copious notes on everything around him, and a perfectionist. Thus he assumed that with his abilities and penchant for details, his organizational skills, and his fearlessness and training, he could make the 92nd a formidable segregated fighting force — that blacks would fall in line, would be inspired by his leadership, and would follow him into war. He believed in the mechanics of training and the smart execution of field exercises where emphasis was placed on tactics and precision. He was a fighter, a man of guts, tenacity, and thoroughness. But he was poor in human relations, demonstrating below average understanding of human psychology, and lacked the skills to motivate and encourage. War and its preparation were mechanical exercises executed by humans who must follow the rules and procedures. It was in the human relations aspect that Almond failed as a commander. His cherished notions of blacks, their inferiority and lack of education, and his recalcitrance to improve basic conditions for them, cast a long shadow over his tenure as commander of the 92nd Infantry Division and eventually led to bitterness and resentment by many of his soldiers. He was overbearing, pushing his men too hard in a context where they felt that they were being used as cannon fodder in the white man's army. And worst of all, he remained aloof from them. That he failed as a battlefield commander and felt bitterly disappointed was not unexpected. The handwriting was on the wall the day he was appointed to command the 92nd Infantry Division.

Conclusion

Lock-stitched into a conceptual framework that embraced the genetic inferiority of the Negro race, and given his cultivated tendencies for the mechanics of war, Almond's command of the 92nd Infantry Division was doomed to failure from its inception. Unyielding in his racist disposition and unwilling to experiment with social conditions confronting blacks within the division, and demonstrating little or no regard to improving those conditions, Almond's leadership created a climate of resentment and low morale. In the mechanics of war, the division was well trained and equipped in spite of the low level of education among most of its enlisted men, and the disparate elements making up its structure. Yet after nineteen months of rigorous training in the United States, beset at times by a multiplicity of varied racial incidents and setbacks, the division's morale was high on the eve of departure to the Mediterranean Theater in Italy. They were looking forward to war and willing to fight. Something was carried over from training and went terribly wrong when the division finally assembled in Italy under General Almond's command — an all-pervading lack of trust. This problem, according to Lee, was the "basic disbelief in the good conscience and the will to do on the part of command toward men, men toward command, and both toward each other."[34] It was a marked feature of the 92nd Division and the commander was ultimately responsible.

Deployment to the War Zone and General Almond's Command

Early in the morning of June 6, 1944, Allied forces finally launched their long-awaited D-Day invasion of the European mainland. It was a momentous day in the American chronicle of World War II, for it not only marked the end of years of arduous training for combat, but it ushered in a new and decisive phase of the war. Thousands of American and Allied soldiers would on this day land on European soil as they stormed ashore on the beaches of Normandy, fighting their way out of the beachhead. It turned into a bloody affair. As they waded to shore hundreds were swiftly cut down by enemy bullets, while thousands made it beyond the shoreline. It was a spectacular yet bloody sight. For an observer looking across the open sea that morning, there appeared suddenly on the near horizon a naval flotilla disgorging tons of human cargo on sandy beaches. But this was no picnic. It was war. With the landing of Allied troops the war had finally entered a new phase, and it marked the beginning of large scale American commitment. Hundreds of thousands of troops would follow, including, in just eight weeks, the first contingent of black American soldiers to arrive on the European continent.

The arrival of lead elements of the 92nd Infantry Division, the first and only all-black division to fight on European soil, marked the beginning of large-scale black combat participation in World War II. And although its mission was mainly defensive, elements of the division were engaged in numerous firefights against an entrenched enemy. The division's deployment and arrival in Italy was piecemeal and occurred in stages during the summer of 1944. So also were its combat operations in that theater, which were characterized by frequent stops, starts, and changes. Its overall performance and quality of its leadership on the other hand were at best debatable. This chapter examines the deployment, reorganization, and combat performance of the 92nd Infantry Division during the period September 1944 through March 1945, just before it launched Operation Second Wind in April 1945.

The examination is not intended to chronicle the division's daily operations, but mainly to ferret out and analyze salient aspects of its performance and leadership — issues of considerable debate and controversy that continue to linger today. In short, we shall attempt to examine closely key aspects of the combat performance of black troops and the failure of their senior white leadership. For it was against this type of background characterized by low morale, deep suspicions and widespread mistrust, and a perception of poor leadership that lieutenants Vernon Baker and John Fox, and to a lesser extent other black soldiers, would rise to the challenge of combat and perform stupendous acts of bravery on the battlefield.

The 370th Combat Team

Prior to his departure from the Louisiana Maneuvers to Fort Huachuca in April 1944, three staff officers from Army Ground Forces Headquarters and the War Department visited General Almond. It was a short but decisive meeting. Almond was informed that a final decision

2. Deployment to the War Zone and General Almond's Command 41

had been made to send one combat team to an overseas theater to represent the 92nd Division. The commander, having interpreted this to mean that only a small faction of the division would be sent overseas and into combat, insisted that the entire 92nd be given the opportunity to fulfill its destiny. After a few exchanges with him over this important issue, the visiting officials accepted Almond's recommendation with the proviso that a combat team would be made ready and sent overseas in advance of the entire division.

The 370th Regimental Combat Team was formed at Fort Huachuca on April 4, 1944, and consisted of the 370th Infantry, the 598th Field Artillery Battalion, and detachments from the division Combat Engineers, Medical, Ordnance, Military Police, Quartermaster and Signal units, and the 92nd Division Headquarters Company. In readying itself for overseas deployment in Italy, the 370th Combat Team was drastically reorganized. Beginning on April 5 and ending on June 28, 1944, it underwent a period of intensive and rigorous training. Men who performed poorly were quickly replaced with others who had better qualifications and demonstrated superior capabilities. In short, the Combat Team represented the best cross-section of men from the division specially selected and trained for combat. And according to the division commander, "It was the best commanded and the best staffed and probably was more fit for early injection into the combat area than any other unit in the division. That's why we selected the combat team 370 to be the first to leave Huachuca."[1] The unit, commanded by Colonel Raymond Sherman, an old friend and confidant of General Almond, was secure in the knowledge that it was "handpicked," well trained, and in excellent physical condition. Their hopes and aspirations and confidence were especially high when they sailed from Hampton Roads, Virginia, on July 15, 1944, for Naples.

But in spite of the handpicked composition of the Combat Team and their intense training and preparation for combat just prior to their departure, General Almond was still plagued with doubts about their "moral attitude toward battle." He was apprehensive about their "mental toughness" and fearful about their "trustworthiness." He knew of their long hours of small arms and tactical training, their deployment and marching abilities, their physical fitness and condition, their strength to command what they controlled, and their dexterity in weapons' utilization, but yet he was uncertain about their upcoming performance in combat.

This combined phenomenon of "uncertainly" and "lack of trust" on his part was part of the larger issue that underscored white commanders' perception of blacks and their ability to be aggressive in combat and their moral attitude toward the battlefield. Would they stand and fight? Or would they cut and run as their predecessors did in World War I? These troubling questions were ever present in the minds of Almond and other senior white commanders of the 92nd Infantry Division. Thirty years later when Almond was asked about his faith in the fighting ability of his men, he curtly replied, "I was uncertain as to what the result would be on entering into combat."[2]

Negro service troops already serving in Italy greeted the news of the arrival of the 370th Combat Team with jubilation. For them, the combat assignment of the 92nd Division represented the culmination of a long and arduous struggle for recognition and equality of treatment — an opportunity to fight for their country as combatants. And so on July 30 when the troopships carrying the 370th arrived alongside Naples harbor, hundreds of black service troops were waiting on the battered docks to welcome the Buffalo Soldiers. Black historian Hondon Hargrove described the scene in these graphic words: "As the thousands of black fighting men, in single file, debarked from the crowded troopships, they presented an impressive and awe-inspiring spectacle. Armed and in full field battle dress, proudly wearing the circular shoulder patch with the black buffalo, they moved smartly and efficiently into their unit formations. As they marched away, every man in step, every weapon in place, chins up and eyes forward, a low rumbling sound came from the troops on the dock, then swelled to a crescendo of thunderous cheering which continued until the last Buffalo unit had disappeared from sight."[3]

Many of these cheering service men, inspired by the spectacular sight of the Black Buffaloes, requested and were later granted transfers to the 92nd Infantry Division. From July 30 until August 23, elements of the 370th Combat Team were busy in orientation programs, resting and readying themselves for battle. Ahead lay the German Gothic Line — an impregnable barrier they must break.

Allied plans in Italy were geared toward piercing the formidable

German Gothic Line. Extending 170 miles across the country and taking maximum advantage of the rugged mountain terrain, the Gothic Line offered the Germans a last hope of defending northern Italy. It began on the Ligurian seacoast near Massa, north of the Arno River, and stretched across the peninsula. Bending southeast from Carrara, through Mount Altissimo and the other coastal hills, it then swung sharply east across the Serchio River Valley and on through the mountains north of Lucca and Pistoia, traversed the upper reaches of the Reno River and swung southeast, then northeast near Pesaro on the Adriatic coast.[4]

The rugged terrain through which this line traversed was marked by an infinite number of broken ridges, spurs, and deep, pocket-shaped valleys that provided a series of excellent defensive positions. To these natural barriers were added a number of fortified defensive structures constructed under direction of skilled German engineers, and extended at various intervals across the line. At some points the line was several miles deep. The shortage of traversable roads made continuous defenses unnecessary, and allowed the concentration of the strongest obstacles at only a few key positions. One observer noted that "These strong points were sprinkled with mine fields, tank traps, concrete-embedded artillery, machine-gun bunkers, antiaircraft guns, and strongly fortified stations for foot traps. Automatic weapons were mutually supporting; their interlocking fields of fire covering wide areas of terrain. Many of the fortifications were carved in the mountainsides, while in some sectors, tank turrets were emplaced in concrete."[5] Thus it was this formidable and very inhospitable terrain that formed the foundation upon which the Gothic Line was built. To German military planners, a successful defense of this line would prevent the Allied forces from reaching and controlling the broad Po Valley, the natural southern approach to the main industrial and agricultural areas of northern Italy.

Attached to the 1st Armored Division, IV Corps, elements of the 370th Combat Team began their battle initiation along the Arno River in the Pontedera area near Pisa on August 23, 1944. Commanded by Major General Willis Crittenberger, IV Corps had the task of defending the greater part of the Fifth Army front that extended thirty miles along the south bank of the Arno River. Its overall objective was to cross the Arno in force and occupy the two major mountains in the Arno Plain: Mount Albano and Mount Pisano. And with an interest in the efficiency of movement of the 370th units and the ability of their men to stay in the combat areas at nights, IV Corps placed them under close scrutiny. After five nights of moving in and out of positions and under close observation, the entire 370th was facing the enemy for the first time. Tension and uncertainty filled the air. None of these black soldiers had ever experienced battle before. But now, they were facing the "real enemy," and for many the "moment of truth had finally arrived."

This beginning phase of the 370th's operations stood in marked contrast to its earlier training history where it had no contact with white troops. Fort Huachuca did not allow for opportunities of integrated training. Blacks trained in isolation at locations far removed from white settlement. Their denial of this vital opportunity to train with white troops and match their skills even for short periods would have augured well for their morale and sense of trust in their white commanders. It did not take the mental perspicacity of a clairvoyant to predict that their performance in actual combat would suffer given this lack of trust in the white commanders who were leading them into battle. But now in the early phase of its combat operations, removed temporarily at least from the stifling and corrosive swirl of domestic politics and segregationist policies, all of its many elements were in intimate contact with American white units, officers, and enlisted men. And what a tremendous difference this enlightened experiment made. Motivated and determined, these black enlisted men and junior officers rose to the challenge and proved themselves as equals to their white counterparts.

During the night of August 27 as it began to feel its way into battle, the Team's 3rd Battalion command post was bombed by enemy aircraft, and two enemy patrols that attacked its position were driven off. Three days later on August 30, a twenty-two-man patrol from Company F crossed the Arno River and confronted the enemy. Led by Lieutenant Jake Chandler and the newly promoted Captain Charles Gandy, the heavily armed patrol crossed the Arno and entered the village of Calcinaia where it destroyed an enemy machine gun position and captured two German soldiers, the first prisoners to be taken by black combat infantrymen in Europe.

The Combat Team's specific mission was to drive the occupying Germans out from Mount Pisano, a mountain mass seven miles wide and ten miles deep, running north and south. On September 1, it joined other elements of IV Corps units to cross the Arno River. Crossing was slow but steady in the face of enemy resistance. And despite many mishaps and a few wounded, the crossing was successful. Effective teamwork by engineers, infantry, and tanks culminated in the capture of Mount Pisano during the evening of September 2. Their training had paid off. The *New York Times* had words of praise for the part played by black soldiers in this small operation:

> The American Fifth Army lashed out in a new offensive today, burst across the Arno on a wide front, seized Pisa and stormed dominating heights on the East in concert with a new drive by the Eighth Army through a 20–mile hold in the Gothic Line. Negro troops of the Ninety Second United States Division, making their first appearance in the battle-line, stormed up the southeast slopes of Mount Pisano, from whose frowning heights the enemy had lobbed shells into the American lines during the long stalemate on this front. The Pisano hill mass lies East and North of Pisa, western anchor of the Gothic Line.[6]

When Mount Pisano fell into American control, the enemy continued to withdraw toward the Gothic Line during the next three days. Their retreat made the advance to Lucca a little easier. The 2nd Battalion, 370th Infantry, crossed the rough trails and steep side of Mount Pisano, reorganized, and commenced its attack toward Lucca on September 4. The ancient walled city of Lucca, famed for the beauty of its classic gardens and its many luxurious mansions, is situated on the south bank of the Serchio River. To the north, the Apennine Mountains rise abruptly from the plains of the Arno. As the only large-sized community in the area, Lucca became the natural focal point for an attacking force advancing to the mountains. Encountering little enemy resistance and moving swiftly, Company E entered Lucca before noon on September 5. Within four hours, Company F joined it. Once Lucca fell into American hands, IV Corps began to regroup its forces and consolidate its positions.

The general advance of Fifth Army and all its attached units toward the Gothic Line commenced in earnest on the morning of September 10. For the next twenty days, the advance made steady progress, covering over two miles per day. When no contacts were made with the enemy, as was the case on the 26th, the advance was more rapid. On that day, patrols of the 370th Combat Team covered a distance in excess of four miles up the Serchio Valley. At the end of the month, marking forty-two days of combat, the 370th Combat Team had advanced approximately twenty-one miles with the 1st Armored Division and IV Corps. It had lost eight men killed in action, including its executive officer, had 248 sick, wounded, or injured, and twenty-three missing or captured — a total loss of 279. And although it had encountered no strong resistance from the enemy, it had advanced beyond the Gothic Line in its sector and cut off Highway 12, the enemy's main east-west route of communications opposite the IV Corps front.[7]

The Combat Team's overall performance was shaky at first but improved steadily toward the end of September. This was their first real battle experience and despite the apprehension among rank and file, there was also a high level of fear and caution. According to one historian, they had skillfully and efficiently made three river crossings and forded many canals and streams under enemy fire. Their units had engaged the enemy in numerous firefights in the villages and in the countryside, clearing nests of snipers, and machine gun posts, and their aggressive patrolling was outstanding enough to win the praise of the IV Corps commander. But more importantly, they had worked closely with white soldiers mainly from the 1st Armored Division, and quickly adjusted to the tank-infantry team assault operations with them.[8] Moreover, they had demonstrated a capacity to operate independently. There were positive signs that the Combat Team, as a whole, was losing the uncertainty that was at first evident when it commenced battle indoctrination two months ago. However, in spite of these encouraging signs, doubts in the minds of senior white leadership began to surface and would eventually cast a dark shadow over the entire campaign.

From the beginning of its entry into battle, there were some signs that units of the 370th Combat Team were neither the most thoroughly trained nor the most thoroughly motivated troops. According to historian Ulysses Lee, "More than a sea voyage was needed to bridge

2. Deployment to the War Zone and General Almond's Command   47

completely the gap between Fort Huachuca and the plain of the Arno."⁹ Many of the faults that they showed were common to new troops: in the first few days they caused more damage to each other than to the enemy; nervous and jittery guards and patrols were more likely to fire at "any noise or anything which moves, and to challenge and fire at about the same time." Loud talking and bunching together were very noticeable among patrols. But these tactical problems were quickly overcome as they settled into the routine of their new environment. There were also signs that the men of the 370th were learning battle lessons. When initially exposed to enemy artillery fire, there was a remarkable tendency among them to leave the danger area by withdrawing to the rear. They soon learned the advantage of getting out of the fire by moving forward. They also learned that a great deal of fire can do relatively little damage. But there were also other developments that contributed toward some aspects of their poor performance: command posts were poorly organized and operated; staffs did not follow standard operating procedures all the time; discipline slackened, with men reasoning that saluting, sanitation, maintenance of weapons, and police orders were not important in the combat zone.

That they were not "aggressive in combat" became the ubiquitous refrain among senior white commanders. While not an idle observation, calculated to belittle and demoralize the fighting ability of black troops, it nevertheless set in motion a train of compelling events that would lead eventually to increasing levels of frustration and "failure." This prevailing lack of confidence in the black soldier's fighting capabilities became the mantra of many senior white commanders. Blacks, under the microscope of white scrutiny, not only lost confidence in their own abilities to fight and display aggression in battle, but also became distrustful of whites and of each other. Thus, the tendency to harbor doubts and gloss over outstanding black combat performance was nothing new among white commanders in the American Army. It was acted out in World War I and became an integral part of the official policy that overshadowed both the recruitment and the utilization of black combat troops during World War II.

However, by the end of September, the combat team commander, Colonel Sherman, expressed satisfaction at the performance of his troops. He was confident that the lessons learned in combat during this early period would prove useful in upcoming contacts with the enemy. The men themselves were convinced that the combat team was far superior to the opposing enemy. A high *esprit de corps* developed among the lower ranks. And while no determined resistance had been met as yet, the men of the 370th Combat Team were ready to fight. Such was the emotional state of these men on October 5 when General Almond arrived in Italy to assume command of the reunited 92nd Infantry Division. As other elements of the division arrived, the Combat Team stood down as a detached 92nd unit and once again became an integral part of the full Division.

The 92nd Infantry Division in Italy: Early Frustrations and Failures

The description and analysis of certain events that follow in this subsection cover only a small part of the 92nd Division's activities in Italy during the last several months of World War II. More detailed accounts are found in Ulysses Lee's *The Employment of Negro Troops*, Hondon Hargrove's *Buffalo Soldiers in Italy*, and Paul Goodman's *A Fragment of Victory*. The attempt here is mainly to examine two major offensive initiatives that were undertaken against the enemy within the first four months since the division's arrival in Italy, and to spotlight the reasons for failure in these operations. This examination is considered useful to an understanding of the negative reports and charges that were later hurled at the men of the division. But before doing that, we pause to consider some relevant geographic and historical background information on Italy, drawn heavily from Paul Goodman's *A Fragment of Victory*.

Geographic Setting

Throughout its long history, Italy's geographic setting and position have had a marked effect on its destiny, and its topographical diversity has, in like manner, influenced the course of its economic, political, and social development. Italy's shape on a map is unmistakable — a high-heeled woman's boot. It is a peninsula that juts out like an extended arm of Europe far into the center of the Mediterranean Sea. "On the East her coast is washed by the waters of the Adriatic Sea; on the South by the Mediterranean. On the West between the mainland and Sicily and Sardinia, is the Tyrrhenian Sea; and further North, in the crook between France and Italy, is the Ligurian Sea."[10] This inland area encompassing the seacoast was the battle sector for the 92nd Infantry Division.

Together with the island of Sicily, Italy almost bridges the waterway separating Europe and Africa — a distance of only ninety miles. Across this strategic intercontinental route many people — rulers, freedmen, and slaves — have marched, migrated, and fought for centuries. But more important, perhaps, than its geographic position as a connecting link between two continents is the advantage Italy holds in commanding the approaches through the busy sea-lanes of communication of the Mediterranean Sea. All east-west shipping must pass along the route between Sicily and North Africa or through the narrow Strait of Messina. Italy controls both of these strategic waterways. The country, therefore, potentially dominates both the western and eastern basins of the Mediterranean.

Geographic position, while one of the very few enduring aspects of international relations, is also relative and its continuing salience depends on economic and military power and historical circumstance. In ancient times when Italy formed the heart of the vast and powerful Roman Empire, her position was so commanding and dominant that all roads led to Rome and all power emanated from the "Eternal City." During the heyday of the Fascist alliance when German armies were steamrolling their opponents, Italy as a non-belligerent exploited her geographic position by blackmailing England and France. Later as an active combatant, she served as the bridge over which the Axis legions crossed into North Africa. But if Italy's geographic position has offered strategic advantages when she has been powerful, it has always been, nevertheless, a vulnerable one. History has demonstrated that the Mediterranean can be a highway for foreign invasion, the proximity to North Africa a danger, and Italy's long and unguarded coastline of some 5,300 miles an inviting target for hostile forces.

An aerial shot of Italy reveals a boot with toe, heel, and a broad kneecap. From north to south, it measures about 760 miles while its width at no point exceeds 150 miles except at the northern junction in the Po Valley where the country widens out to 350 miles. The area of Italy, including the islands of Sicily and Sardinia, is only 119,733 square miles, about twice the size of Florida and over 20,000 square miles larger than Great Britain. There is an absence of vast plains or boundless steppes. No flat, sweeping grassland greets the eye. Large open expanses are nowhere in sight, thus making impossible a war of movement with wide columns of tanks and follow-on ground forces. In Italy space cannot be sold to gain time because there is not enough space to sell. What space there is, however, is for the most part extremely rugged and must be bought at a terrible price, as the men of the 92nd Infantry Division and others who have fought for ground in Italy have learned the hard way.

Mountains, steep and rugged, dominate the length of the land. In a vast concave to the north tower the magnificent Alps. The Ligurian Apennines that follow the semicircle of the Gulf of Genoa turn southeast and run parallel to the coast before merging with the central and southern Apennines. These two ranges extend like a huge spinal cord down the entire length of the peninsula to the toe of the boot, and after a break at the narrow Strait of Messina, through Sicily. Thrusting transversely across the peninsula are stark, jagged ridges crumpled one upon another in fifty-mile depth with sheer up-thrust walls of solid stone. This geologic reality combined with winding gorges slashed by centuries of erosion would hinder the advance of any invader. On the upper slopes of the mountains, wherever soil exists, scrub oak and pine cling to the barren slopes. For the most part, though, the massive hills are bare rock, gashed into precipitous ridges and deep-pocketed valleys. High above, dozens of solitary peaks rear snow-capped summits over the honeycombed panorama below. Here and there the Apennines spread out into numerous subsidiary chains which not only give Italy a beautiful and variegated landscape, but which also divide the country into numerous and separate geographic entities, a condition ideal for the development of pockets of culture and provincialism.

Italy's network of roads, mainly narrow and tortuously winding, frequently become military bottlenecks. The state highways are mostly satisfactory but the few secondary and heavily traveled east-west roads within the peninsula are inferior by comparison. Steep beyond belief, these roads curve in never-ending series of horseshoe bends and are channeled through narrow defiles. Italian engineers had done a masterful job of cutting and building roads through and around mountains. Years later, they would employ these very skills in carving out roads along the twisting and tortuously winding ridges along the Atlantic coasts of Cape Town, South Africa. Landslides frequently put these Italian roads out of commission. And in many areas of the Apennines they were sometimes reduced to mere cart tracks and mule trails.

Rivers and valleys in the peninsula have always played an important strategic role in times of war. For the most part, these rivers are not navigable waterways. Many are torrential, becoming raging floods during the spring thaws. Two rivers, the Tiber and the Arno, have the greatest historical significance. The Tiber rises between the northern and central Apennines, parallels the mountains southward for about fifty miles, crawls its way among the Sabine Hills, then passes through Rome and finally empties into the Tyrrhenian Sea. The Arno also has its source in the northern and central Apennines. Sweeping around in a great horseshoe curve, it passes through the beautiful city of Florence, irrigates the Florentine plain, and continues westward to enter the sea at Marina di Pisa. Many smaller rives cut sharply down from the central mountain mass and empty their waters either into the Adriatic on the east or the Tyrrhenian Sea on the west. Between the spur of the Alps lie seven beautiful lakes. Crisscrossing the Italian landscape are numerous narrow valleys that make military movements difficult and tax the skill of the best engineers. The terrain overwhelmingly favors the defense and is ideal for digging in and delaying actions, a condition that the Germans took advantage of and exploited to the fullest. For an invader, the landscape is as much a foe as it is an enemy. This fact would resonate with the Allied forces throughout the Mediterranean campaign in World War II. It was also a fact not lost on the 92nd Infantry Division.

The popular conception of Italy as a land of smiling sunshine and soft, warm days is misleading and an oversimplification. Not only are there great differences between the climate of northern and southern

Italy, there are also many different geographic areas. Location and topographical formations condition its weather. Whereas northern Italy experiences cold winter temperatures, southern Italy enjoys a warm, Mediterranean type climate as that of Greece or Spain. And though palms grow in Venice, in the provinces of Abruzzi and Molise there are frequent snows and raw, blustery days. Indeed, the central range of the Apennines has some of the coldest districts in all Italy with snow falling in early November and storms occurring as late as May.

Throughout the peninsula, summers are generally hot and dusty while the winters, particularly in the mountainous areas in the north, are cold and wet. The winter season also brings a good deal of fog and cloudy weather with poor visibility, which makes low flying and air support operations, especially among the mountains, exceedingly dangerous. The autumn and spring rains are treacherous and even violent. It is then that the countryside becomes a sea of mud, the plains a soggy mass, the rivers unfordable, and even the creeks raging torrents. Italy's weather is by no stretch of the imagination a friend of military operations. Neither is its geographic landscape. Its geographic and meteorological conditions would also overhang the 92nd Infantry Division like the sword of Damocles, frustrating their advances and exacting a heavy toll on morale and manpower.

Historical Retrospect

Italy was a battleground of the ancient world. Divided and dismembered for centuries, it did not exist as a unified country until 1870. Until A.D. 476, the history of Italy was largely the history of ancient and Imperial Rome when military might was at its height and when all roads led to Rome.

The Samnite Wars, which brought the peninsula under the domination of Rome, and the Punic Wars, which saw Hannibal, the North African military leader, cross the impassable Alps to win his famous victory at Cannae over 200 years before the birth of Christ in Bethlehem, were fought on Italian soil. It was in Italy that Caesar crossed the Rubicon and defeated the army of his rival Pompey. During the height

2. Deployment to the War Zone and General Almond's Command   53

of the Roman Empire when the Caesars reigned as gods, proud legionaries marched the length and breadth of the land. With the tramp of the foot soldier and the clanging of swords and shields, the Roman military was a ubiquitous sight. That the strength of Rome and its capability to dominate lies in its military prowess was not an exaggeration.

Rome was the quintessence of a true garrison state, a condition that would also lead to its decline and fall. Historian Edward Gibbon summed up Rome's decline as a world power thus:

> The decline of Rome was the natural and inevitable effect of immoderate greatness. Prosperity ripened the principle of decay; the cause of the destruction multiplied to the extent of conquest; and, as soon as time or accident had removed the artificial supports, the stupendous fabric yielded to the pressure of its own weight. The story of the ruin is simple and obvious; and instead of inquiring why the Roman Empire was destroyed, we should be surprised that it had subsided so long.[11]

During the fifth century when the proud and impregnable edifice of the Empire was crumbling on every hand, when apathy among Roman citizens reigned supreme, barbarian tribes from the north moved in to plunder and pillage. In 410 the Visigoths swept into the Empire, pushed southward into central Italy and sacked Rome, burning, looting, and destroying everything in their path. Later the Huns from Central Asia, tough fighters on wiry ponies, pressed westward under the indomitable leadership of Attila to the Po Valley in 452. The Vandals, who had earlier invaded Africa through France and Spain, crossed the narrow span of water into Italy and stormed Rome in 455 — the second time the city had been pillaged within a half century.

The medieval period brought the same tragic panorama of conflict and struggle to Italy. The triumph of the Germanic leader Odoacer, who took over the government of Rome in 476, lasted barely twelve years when another Teutonic chieftain, Theodoric, drove into northern Italy at the end of the fifth century with 100,000 Ostrogoths and set up a powerful kingdom. In the sixth century the ambitious Byzantine Emperor Justinian re-conquered Italy after a long and bitter struggle. A few years later a new wave of Germans, the Lombards, poured into northern Italy, overran most of the country, and established a kingdom that lasted until 774, when Charlemagne, the great leader of the Franks, wrested from them the northern part of the peninsula. The southern portion was lost to the Saracens in 827. After Charlemagne's death in 814, Italy was divided among the Lombards to the north, the Papal States in the center, and the Byzantines and Arab Muslims to the south. Norman adventurers returning from pilgrimages to the Holy Land in Palestine assisted the southern Italians in throwing off the Byzantine and Saracen yoke, but ended by setting up the Norman kingdom of Naples and Sicily.

Most of the modern period witnessed a repetition of the tragedy that had engulfed Italy during the medieval era. For a time though, city-states such as Venice and Genoa became economically prosperous, but they too soon fell to warring one against the other until league was pitted against league and principality against principality in the struggle for the balance of power within the peninsula. Then came in rapid succession a number of foreign invasions—Charles VIII of France in 1494, and Charles V, the Holy Roman Emperor early in the sixteenth century—which left the country in a state of feudalistic disunity. France and the Spanish and Austrian Hapsburgs contended for control over the peninsula. And the ensuing conflict between these powers lasted for several centuries. It finally reached its zenith in 1796 when Napoleon crossed the Ligurian Alps and defeated the Austrians in northern Italy. In 1800 he repeated this feat at Marengo, descending upon Italy with his army through the pass of the Great St. Bernard, and on May 26, 1805, crowned himself king of Italy.

Following the collapse of the Napoleonic regime, Italy once again fell under the control of the Hapsburgs. But it was not until the revolutions of 1848 and the Austro-Sardinian War of 1859 when Napoleon III allied himself with the upstart Italian state, that the shackles of foreign domination finally began to weaken. In 1861 Italy became a united kingdom. Nine years later in 1870 when the French left Rome, the peninsula became a unitary state for the first time in its long history of struggles with foreign domination. Italy's participation on the Allied side in World War I added to the background of struggle and war that had raged within the peninsula for centuries. And many of the conflicts chronicled here took place on the same terrain over which the 92nd Infantry Division fought in World War II. And it was also on this terrain marked by numerous acts of struggle and triumph, of pain and suffering, of victory and defeat, and of valor and death, that lieutenants Baker and Fox of the 92nd Infantry Division would display a level of gallantry that would earn them the nation's highest award for valor in combat — the Medal of Honor.

Internal Problems

The drive for Massa, one of the division's major objectives, began the day after General Almond's arrival at the division's headquarters in Viareggio, a seaside resort on the Ligurian coast. It would set a pattern for future operations and bring to the fore all the latent problems confronting the division and its leadership. Indeed, Massa would also test the mettle of black combat capabilities and preparation.

Attacking abreast toward Mount Cauala, the first of a series of heights guarding the southern approach to Massa, elements of the division failed repeatedly in their efforts to seize and hold the objective. In a downpour, slogging through a sea of mud, the 370th Infantry advanced about a mile while the 2nd Armored Group, operating on the left flank, made little progress in the face of continual enemy artillery fire. Resuming the next day, the attack continued, but with no success. On the third day, October 8, 1944, two battalions of the 370th started up the mountain again but quickly retreated in the face of heavy mortar and artillery fire. On the morning of the following day, two companies of the 2nd Battalion made a bold attempt to reach the summit of Mount Cauala. Trying a different route, they began their ascent up the less precipitous east side under cover of darkness at 3 a.m. Historian Ulysses Lee described what happened soon after sunrise: "By 0830, taking ten prisoners on the way up, they were at the top of the mountain. By noon heavy machine gun and mortar fire had pushed them about one third of the way back; by late evening the two companies, under fire from both flanks and from the front and believing they were in danger of being cut off from the rear, withdrew without orders to Seravezza."[12] This pattern of attack and withdrawal would continue for several more days. It led to mounting frustrations among rank and file, no less among senior white commanders.

Confronted for the first time since its arrival in Italy with determined German resistance, elements of the 92nd Infantry Division netted a gain of only 8,000 yards in six days and failed to seize and hold their objective while sustaining over 400 casualties. Compared with its earlier battle indoctrination along the plains of the Arno where the 370th did relatively well, its performance one week later when it was ordered to attack and seize the high ground proved troublesome, difficult, and costly. This failure to capture an enemy stronghold would set in motion a pattern for the division's combat operations throughout the war. It repeated itself as one after another of the units became involved in similar occurrences. And it was this pattern of repeated failure on the battlefield that would eventually shape the dispositions of whites towards black combat capabilities. The problems did not manifest themselves suddenly; they were already deeply entrenched well before the division moved overseas.

Evidences of a growing malaise among officers and men began to manifest themselves on the first day of the attack. They continued to plague the division throughout the month, as one after another of its units went up the slopes of Mount Cauala and other heights and came down again for an infinite variety of reasons ranging from poor organization, lack of control, and panic to weakness in offensive operations, communications failure, and stiffer enemy resistance.

The attack on the night of October 9 was but one example of this emerging pattern of failure. After three daylight attempts to capture and occupy Mount Cauala, a night attack was then decided upon. The advancing company was able to cut through enemy wire without a shot. "When well into position," according to one eyewitness account, "it encountered light fire, perhaps from a machine gun, a machine pistol, and a rifle, and the company streamed back through the wire and back across the Sera River despite the efforts of its officers to control it. By morning, ten men and two officers remained dejectedly alone, across the river, opposite their objective. The company was rounded up and reorganized. Again, on the night of October 12, when other units, using scaling ladders, had again taken Mount Cauala, this company had been able to get no more than thirty men started. Mount Cauala was lost again."[13]

Typical of the various explanations advanced for the failure to capture Mount Cauala was one offered by a black company commander who made a fourth attempt to take his men to the summit: "They will not stay in their positions unless constantly watched and give as their reason for leaving the fact that the men next to them will leave anyway so there is no reason for them to stay.... The few good officers and noncommissioned officers in the company are not able to carry the load placed on them, no matter how hard they work. Morale is bad and I dread to make a night move, because so many of the men can slip away."[14] General Almond's explanation for the repeated failure of elements of the division to advance and hold the forward position was their woeful weakness to be aggressive on the offensive. They lacked, in his estimation, the guts to fight with tenacity and determination. Moreover, he felt that the men of the division were not capable of a combat offense. Like so many of his senior commanders, Almond did not understand and appreciate the root cause of the problem confronting the men under his command.

The deep-seated, recalcitrant problem that undermined the division's performance in battle could be traced to the "wavering faith of commanders in the ability and determination of subordinates and enlisted men, and the continuation in the minds of enlisted men of training period convictions that they could not trust their leaders."[15] This problem of distrust, though pervasive throughout the ranks and devastating to morale and singleness of purpose, did not prevent the display of individual acts of courage and heroism. In the various attempts to capture and hold Mount Cauala, the one on the morning of October 12 was particularly noteworthy for its display of bravery. Though pinned down by enemy fire for several hours, Companies F and I held their positions. Captain Gandy, commander of Company F, though mortally wounded, held out until 3 o'clock the following morning when the units withdrew on regimental orders. A platoon of Company L fought off eight enemy counterattacks on Mount Strettoia while awaiting reinforcement from another company that failed to find its position. This platoon held its position until it ran out of ammunition. This remarkable display of individual leadership and bravery did not go unnoticed. Reporting to the division commander about these instances of gallantry, Lt. Col. John Phelan, the newly appointed executive officer of the 370th Infantry Regiment and a veteran of the Italian campaign, noted: "During my period of observation, I have heard of just as many acts of individual heroism among Negro troops as among white. There is no reason to believe that there is any greater lack of individual guts among them."[16]

If the division's effort to capture and hold Mount Cauala proved difficult and elusive, then its attempt to dislodge the enemy from the Serchio Valley and cross the Cinquale Canal four months later was even more horrendously difficult and costly. The positions held by the Germans in the Serchio Valley and along the flat coastal plain of the Cinquale Canal were among the most formidable defenses along the Gothic Line. The loss of these positions would clear the way for the American Fifth Army forces to capture the naval base at La Spezia, and then permit a wide open advance to important enemy installations in mid-northern Italy and the Po Valley. German efforts to hold these positions would prove costly to American troops, and of much more significance, would test the will and combat effectiveness of the 92nd Infantry Division. It happened during four days of bitter fighting February 8–11, 1945. The end result would lead not only to a strong pronouncement by higher headquarters of the Division's inability to be aggressive and strong in offensive operations, but also to its complete reorganization.

On February 8, the 92nd Division conducted Operation Fourth Term — a coordinated but short-lived attack to seize the Strettoia hill mass dominating the coastal plain, cross the Cinquale Canal, and advance up the Serchio Valley to the Lama di Sotto Ridge. This three-pronged attack had all the earmarks of a major offensive. Medium and light fighter-bombers of the XXII Tactical Air Command, naval guns, medium and light tanks, tank destroyers, and the usual infantry, artillery, and supporting troops participated. A task force was organized and designated Task Force 1. It consisted of the 3rd Battalion, 366th Infantry Regiment; 760th Tank Battalion; 84th Chemical Mortar Battalion; Company B, 317th Engineering Battalion; and the 27th Field Artillery Battalion; and other smaller elements. Commanded by Lieutenant Colonel Edward Rowney, Task Force 1's zone of operation extended from Highway 1 left to the Ligurian Sea, over the large marsh area and the Cinquale Canal. It was ordered to advance along the beach, cross the Cinquale Canal near its mouth, then turn inland toward Highway 1. On paper this operation appeared quite straightforward, but its execution was mired in difficulties and led to mounting frustrations.

At 6 a.m. the attack began after intense artillery and chemical mortar preparation. Watching from an observation post were General Almond, General Mark Clark, commander of the 15th Army Group, and General Lucian Truscott, Fifth Army commander. A slight mist prevailed with low scattered cloudiness. The haze still permitted visibility to six miles in the mountains and up to twelve miles in the coastal area. To conceal the forward movements of the advancing tanks, large volumes of smoke were intermingled with high explosives and fire from infantry weapons and tank destroyers. Moving rapidly across the wide expanse of no-man's land and in spite of scattered mines, the attacking force covered hundreds of yards of ground within the first hour.

While the 371st Infantry was jabbing at Mount Folgorito on the right and the 370th was experiencing considerable difficulties in the center at the base of the Strettoia hill mass, Task Force 1 on the left was struggling with difficulties and bogged down by enemy fire. And although the main effort of the three-pronged attack was concentrated by the 370th Infantry near Strettoia, the operation in the flat, soggy terrain at the Cinquale Canal by Task Force 1 had more problems and drama and attracted most of the attention. It was here that the most severe opposition developed. The enemy had rightly calculated to concentrate most of its firepower on this approaching sector. Besides fire from small arms from the German 148th Fusilier Battalion and supporting mortars and artillery, the attacking elements of Task Force 1 encountered a constant barrage of heavy and accurate fire from the big coastal guns located at Punta Bianca in the La Spezia area.

Roughly waist-deep and ninety feet wide at its mouth, the Cinquale was a small, meandering canal with a delta to its south. Rehearsal for the crossing took a week and revealed the need for intensive preparation. Promptly at 5 a.m. on February 7, the first attacking wave of Task Force 1 shoved off to a successful start. As it approached the mouth of the canal severe problems began to develop. The task force commander who had written in detail about this operation related the situation:

> I was pleased to find that the tank crews of both the disabled tanks stayed with their tanks and continued to fire down the canal covering the movement of troops across the canal. As far as I could tell there had not been a single casualty up to this point. While I was comforting myself with this thought, the first of several long-range shells from the Punta Bianca naval guns near La Spezia began to land right in the mouth of the canal. The first one hit squarely in the middle of my little command group and when I looked around there were only two others who had not been hit. The shell had killed seven. The entire mouth of the canal appeared to turn red with blood.[17]

Wave after wave of attacking elements of the task force was beaten back. Disabled tanks and wreckage were strewn everywhere. And compounding the carnage inflicted by a determined enemy was the immediate resurfacing of panic and straggling among the men of the task force.

The problem of handling men as they fled from their forward positions to the rear was acute throughout the division's history in combat. Repeated efforts to cross the Cinquale Canal would exacerbate this problem and bring it into sharper focus. During this short operation, General Almond directed the establishment of a straggler line that was manned on the first day by one officer and twenty military police. By the third day, it rose to two officers and sixty-two police. In all, the division's straggler line handled a total of 751 men within a three-day period. Between November 1, 1944, and May 12, 1945, 2,184 stragglers were apprehended. Because of the nature of the Italian terrain, the many exits from the front line through mountain passes in the areas in which the 92nd Division operated, and the many tiny villages and isolated houses scattered throughout the area, it was nearly impossible to maintain an efficient straggler line. Many soldiers seemed content to hide in houses in the vicinity and set up housekeeping there. The severity of the problem led to swift action by the division's command. Almond felt that the solution was not to put the straggler in the stockade in the rear, but promptly return him to the front line under guard escort and put him in action again. This strategy, to some extent, stopped the straggling and its use was continued until the war's end in May 1945.

Analysis of the Cinquale Canal fiasco laid the blame squarely on the enlisted men of the division and their platoon commanders. A closer examination of this debacle, however, would reveal another story. While certainly not the most difficult of military operations undertaken in World War II, it was nevertheless fraught with poor planning and mediocre strategy from the onset. Lacking in natural cover, the coastal areas along the canal and particularly at the point of crossing left the men and tanks of Task Force 1 highly visible targets. In addition, the mouth of the canal where the crossing was attempted several times was within the range of heavy, accurate, and concentrated enemy gunfire. The Italian naval guns at La Spezia included six 152mm and four 128mm fixed coastal guns. And nowhere along the Gothic Line had American or Allied troops been within range of such accurate, heavy, and devastating ordnance. In a letter to General Truscott, Almond acknowledged the presence of these guns and their accuracy:

> The Coastal batteries on Punta Bianca are among the enemy's chief harassing agencies in the coastal sector, and is one of the threats against our advance — these guns are accurately registered on all key points along the coast and have proven their ability to deliver extremely effective fire on our positions without fear of retaliation.[18]

The acting chief of staff of the division also admitted to the devastating impact these guns had on Task Force 1 during the operation of February 8-11. His report, attached to Almond's letter, asserted that "These guns are protected by mines, light and heavy anti-aircraft guns, wire, and emplaced machine guns, and it is not believed that raids on the positions could be successful.... Many dive-bomb missions have failed to impair the effectiveness of these guns as was particularly evident during the action of 8-11 February, when their fire was singularly effective. These guns are causing damage to our front lines—now, and if not destroyed, will cause damage to any advance we make."[19] That they were used with great effect against black soldiers of Task Force 1 is not in question. To many of the survivors of that operation, the continuous fire from these coastal guns was one of the most terrifying and destructive factors in the enemy's defense. According to one survivor, Lieutenant Dennette Harrod of the 366th Infantry Regiment, "The sound of gunfire from Punta Bianca never ceased and the sound and the sight of the heavy shells falling and exploding among us was terrifying."[20]

In addition, the terrain along the coastal plain lent itself to maximum defense capabilities that were adroitly exploited by the enemy. Crisscrossing the operational sector of Task Force 1 were dozens of smaller, natural canals and creeks, man-made drainage, and irrigation ditches. The presence of large volumes of water left the ground constantly soft and mushy, thereby making it difficult for tanks and other vehicles to maneuver effectively. Moreover, thousands of mines were laid on roads, trails, paths, and ditches. The Cinquale was literally a minefield. The beaches were also heavily mined. And the synergistic effect of all these natural and man-made impediments was to force the attacking troops to advance directly into areas where the most concentrated and effectively destructive firepower could be brought to bear against them, day or night. During the attack of February 8–11, the German strategy proved to be just that.

Under these prevailing conditions the results of this operation along the canal should have surprised no one. General Almond was well aware of enemy dispositions. Moreover, he had reconnoitered the area days before launching the crossing and was therefore very familiar with the terrain and its setbacks. This fiasco could have been avoided had more time and preparation been given to planning and execution. Given the same set of geographic and military circumstances, the results likely would have been precisely the same had the attacking force been white and not black. To lay the blame, therefore, squarely on the shoulders of the enlisted men and junior leaders of the division was clearly an abdication of responsible leadership, and not the last that would be seen in the campaign.

Reorganization and General Almond's Command

Operation Fourth Term, concluded in mid–February when the attack on the Strettoia hill mass and the crossing of the Cinquale Canal was called off, exposed the rigidities and weaknesses in the division's offensive capabilities, and at the same time called attention to its internal organization and leadership. This recent experience combined with a knowledge of its past led many senior white officers to believe that the division was incapable of executing a sustained offensive action. On the second day of Operation Fourth Term, General Truscott, Fifth Army Commander who was sharing an observation post with General Almond, advised that the attack be called off immediately. His advice fell on deaf ears. General Almond was not about to cave in yet. He held his ground and allowed the operation to continue into the third day before he finally called it off. Almond was well aware of the heavy casualties the division was sustaining in this offensive and knew that little or no progress was being made in the advance. He also acknowledged that the "offensive capabilities of the division were sadly lacking."[21] In spite of these serious misgivings and in the face of a rapidly deteriorating situation, he continued the attack knowing that his men would continue to be slaughtered in large numbers.

The important point in any analysis of this tragic military engagement was Almond's readiness to place blame for the operation's failure on his lower rank officers and enlisted men. "The reason for the failure," Almond explained to General Truscott, "was due almost entirely to the unreliability of the infantry units as shown by their repeated withdrawals in the face of enemy fire and small, though determined, hostile counterattacks; the withdrawals by our infantry, take the forms of panics, or disorderly retirements with little heed to command and leadership, particularly the weak leadership in the platoon echelons. Little if any determined offensive spirit to meet the enemy at close quarters existed in most of the infantry units."[22] At the same time, Almond had nothing but praise for the division's white regimental and battalion commanders. In his view, the soldiers—black enlisted men and platoon leaders—were responsible for the failure.

It was against this background characterized by poor combat

performance by enlisted men on the one hand, and an incapacity for sustained offensive action by the division on the other, that finally led to a decision for the division's reorganization. Unnoticed and unspoken at the time, but equally credible, was the crucial issue of General Almond's poor leadership. His fitness and suitability to continue to lead black troops went unquestioned among white senior commanders. But among the rank and file of the division, including black officers, he was viewed very differently, and considered a mediocre strategist and ineffective military leader. Hargrove makes the point that had the opinions or recommendations of black officers been sought before the decision was made to reorganize, "It is certain that the consensus would have been that General Almond and his staff should be held fully responsible for the alleged 'poor performance' of his command, and therefore relieved of it and replaced by another commander. It is equally certain that such a recommendation, had it been submitted would have been ignored."[23]

When the 15th Army Group planned for the upcoming spring offensive, scheduled to start in early April, they felt that it was absolutely necessary that the entire Fifth Army be able to maintain a sustained, offensive operation. The ability to maintain such an offensive attitude was regarded as critical to success. Every outfit was judged against this criterion. Sadly, the bruised and battered condition of the 92nd Infantry Division after Operation Fourth Term convinced the army group command that in its present state, the division could not be relied upon to accomplish the tasks of sustaining an offensive attitude in the coastal sector and capturing La Spezia at the proper time, without a significant structural reorganization. The Group also felt that there were not sufficient organized troops available to permit the reduction of the 92nd Division to a secondary role. However, the need to retain the division as a unit was also widely recognized. And to discard it at this crucial juncture of the war would have proven disastrous to General Almond's reputation and future career in the Army.

Soon after the February attack, General George Marshall, chief of staff of the Armed Forces and chairman of the Joint Chiefs of Staff who had been visiting with General Eisenhower in France at the time, decided to visit Italy and learn first hand about the 92nd Division's poor combat performance. He had heard about the Cinquale fiasco and wanted to help out his old friend. Accompanying him on this important visit were General Truscott, the Army commander, General Crittenberg, the Corps commander, and General Mark Clark, the Army Group commander. His arrival found Almond and other senior officers of the division in deep conference, contemplating the consequences of reorganization and precisely how it should be done. Reminiscing on the scene thirty years later, General Almond recalled: "When General Marshall arrived at my command post, he looked at me with an eagle eye and said, 'You have had a heck of a time in the last two weeks, haven't you?' I said, 'Yes General, you can rely on that.' He then said, 'If you had some reorganization in this division, would it help you if I sent the Japanese-American Regiment known as the 442 Infantry Regiment to be attached to this Division?' I said, 'Anything you did in that manner would help me. It would be particularly desirable to have you send the Japanese-American Regiment to assist me in any way possible. I understand that this regiment is very reliable in a combat way, particularly its 100th battalion that has demonstrated great heroism in all occasions.' General Marshall said, 'Then that will be done. You can expect them to arrive within the next 10 days from the Seventh Army area in France.'"[24] Almond was ecstatic.

Moreover, General Marshall's idea about the precise nature of the reorganization led the way to a resolution of the problem confronting General Almond and his senior staff. He proposed that the most reliable elements of the three organic infantry regiments of the division be used to form one combat regiment, and that the remaining two regiments—the 365th and 371st—be replaced by the 473rd and the 442nd Infantry Regiments. The 473rd Infantry, a predominantly white regiment, would be available for immediate use in the coastal sector, while the 442nd—a Japanese-American Infantry Regiment—would be recalled from southern France. To strengthen the 370th Infantry, dozens of officers and more than 1,300 enlisted men—the most proficient soldiers from the 365th and 371st were transferred into the 370th. Marshall not only helped the division commanders solve their reorganization problem, but he also made available to them the 442nd Japanese-American Infantry Regiment, one of the best in all of World War II and a regiment that he was particularly proud of.

Needless to say, General Almond was elated and felt that this would be the salvation of the 92nd Division combat capability. It was also his own salvation as a division commander. In a statement to Major General Alfred Gruenther, chief of staff, 15th Army Group, Almond concurred that "The divisional potentiality will be greatly increased by the use of the 442nd and 473rd Infantry Regiments." He went on to add: "I do not visualize appreciable difficulties in their employment with our troops."[25] The Japanese-American Regiment, the stepchild of General Marshall, was famed for its tenacity, aggressiveness, and superb fighting ability. He described them as "spectacular" and ordered that they be decorated, or he will do it himself. Almond was also impressed with the 442nd Infantry Regiment. He had nothing but praise for their utmost dedication to executing offensive action in the face of stiff enemy resistance, and felt that their presence would make a great difference in his theater of operation. After the war ended, General Almond, on his way to the United States, stopped over in Frankfurt to see General Eisenhower. Discussing freely the various aspects of the war, General Eisenhower jokingly said to Almond, "If I'd had you in my control about two months ago, I'd have wrung your neck." "Why?" laughed Almond. "Because I lost to you in Italy the best regiment from the 7th Army in France, much to my disappointment because of the fine combat qualities of that regiment [the 442nd]," replied Eisenhower.

The proposal for the division's reorganization also called for the removal of the all-black 366th Infantry Regiment from the front lines. It was detached from the division and eventually converted into a general service engineer unit "without occasioning any comment whatever," because the need for engineers had been amply demonstrated by the conversion of antiaircraft units, the use of Italian engineers, and the employment of civilians. By organizing two general service regiments, all personnel of the 366th could be utilized which prevented the return of any of them to replacement depots from which they could be routed back individually into the reorganized 92nd Division. This was an astute tactical move by Almond. The removal of the 366th regiment from the 92nd Division structure would neither create any manpower shortages nor present any further "headaches" for senior white commanders. General Almond was determined to fashion out of this restructuring exercise a reorganized division with a numerically smaller amount of black infantry combatants. With General Marshall's blessings, he saw an opportunity that, if executed correctly, could redeem his already tarnished and faltering leadership.

The plan, finally approved by 15th Army Group, directed that the reorganized 92nd Division be prepared for a limited objective attack in the coastal sector at the earliest predictable date and that, for security reasons, no publicity should be given to the reorganization of the division.[26] By mid–March, all transfers were completed, and the newly reorganized division presented a "Rainbow Coalition" of forces on the eve of the final offensive in the Italian campaign. It included:

- the 473rd Infantry, a white regiment;
- the 442nd Infantry, a Japanese-American regiment;
- the 370th Infantry, a "new" black regiment with racially mixed officers;
- organic artillery and service units that were black;
- the 758th (black) and 760th (white) tank battalions; and
- the 679th (black) and 894th (white) tank destroyer battalions.

The reorganized Division, along with the rest of Fifth Army, began the final offensive of the war in Italy on April 5, 1945. The 92nd was no longer a Negro division. Of its seven "combat" elements, only three were black with one being a regular infantry regiment. In sum, the reorganization radically changed the division's composition and strengthened its combat offensive capabilities. From this point on, the division performed extremely well, particularly the 442nd and 473rd regiments. The performance of the "new" black regiment, the 370th Infantry, was satisfactory after a very shaky start. They were utilized as flank protection, and reserved for use after the enemy had been dislodged from his entrenched positions.

Evaluation and Conclusion

"Full of beans and vinegar" when he took command of the 92nd Infantry Division, General Ned Almond was confident that he was going to make this outfit one of the greatest units in the Army. With his talent, disciplined approach to tasks, and capacity for hard work, he felt that he could convert these black soldiers into a formidable segregated fighting force. After all, he was tough, and considered a great fighter. General William McCaffrey, who was his chief of staff during World War II in Italy, described Almond as a "tremendously organized man. Every night, no matter how tired he was, he sat down and wrote a summary of what he had done that day. He had his aides keeping notes as he went around. He really knew how to command."[27] Almond was a model military officer after the German tradition — disciplined, incredibly organized, fearless, and highly motivated. The Army took priority in his life. But by mid–March 1945, nearly two months before the war came to an end in Italy and five months after he assumed full operational command of the division; Almond felt let down by his men and bitterly disappointed by their mediocre combat performance. Their continued failure to engage the enemy and hold ground played right into his conceptual framework about black soldiers.

He turned his disappointment into crafting a profile of the Negro soldier and officer — a profile based more on considerations of racial characteristics than on sound judgment and closer observation. To General Almond the Negro officer was a by-product of his race, and as such perpetuates the same characteristics in the Army to a large extent that he did in civilian life. Because of lower economic level, he lacks pride in himself and pride of accomplishment. "Servility," Almond went on to say, "has been bred in him for generations, therefore, he does not develop into an aggressive troop leader; his aggressiveness, if any, usually manifests itself in the rear areas or along race-conscious lines.... The Negro officer, in general, fails to meet minimum infantry combat standards. He lacks pride, aggressiveness, and a sense of responsibility and has practically no command capacity above the grade of captain. His race consciousness seriously affects his general efficiency."[28]

In his description of the Negro noncommissioned officer and enlisted soldier, Almond was even more mordant in his pronouncement. "The Negro noncommissioned officer," he believed, "cannot be developed in self-confidence and consequent leadership within reasonable time for emergency infantry combat use. He lacks pride, is careless and undependable, and cannot induce enlisted men under his command to follow him in danger — principally because he himself is afraid of infantry combat.... The Negro soldier," he asserted, "lacks pride and trust in his fellow soldier. He distorts facts, is unreliable and fears the 'unseen' such as the enemy at night and enemy artillery or mortar fire."[29]

While the above descriptions are clearly prejudicial and flowed unmistakably from his personal bitterness and disappointment with black troops in combat, they nevertheless revealed Almond's impression of, and regard and disposition toward Negroes. He could not bring himself to see Negroes as full human beings capable of undertaking and performing the same tasks as whites. Segregation was cultural with him and he made every effort to keep the races apart even while in Italy. He was seen as overbearing in his demeanor and unreasonable in his demands of people. While on the one hand he expected much from his men, he was not prepared on the other hand to treat them with respect, to encourage their efforts, to build trust and confidence in his leadership, and more importantly, to mitigate the impact of segregation and ameliorate their condition on the battlefield. These behavioral dispositions were transparent and were readily perceived by his troops. They inevitably led to widespread distrust among enlisted men and junior officers of the division. And it was this phenomenon of "distrust" that General Almond had failed to understand and come to grips with in his leadership of black troops.

But apart from these personal and professional characteristics, Almond also demonstrated a serious lack of military leadership. His plans, whether for patrols or major operations, were not only very secretive and developed far in advance, but were rarely transmitted to those who had need of the knowledge. Seldom did small units and individual soldiers have any knowledge of what was planned for units operating to their immediate right or left, and seldom did they themselves know what the general plan intended to accomplish. And when alternatives were provided, as was the case on several occasions, they were completely unknown. For example, when the division made its February 1945 attack after long and detailed planning, not even the assistant section chiefs in G-2 and G-3 knew that the attack was going to be made until a few hours before troops crossed the line of departure. In almost all of the operations undertaken by the division, detailed plans—down to the platoon level—were developed and prescribed by Almond, an approach that clearly stifled initiative and flexibility of small unit commanders. His micro-management style was too overbearing and it ineluctably led to widespread resentment and mistrust.

The overall combat performance of the 92nd Infantry Division in Italy during World War II, while at best mediocre, was nevertheless outstanding for its individual acts of heroism and bravery. And while its mission was mainly defensive, it nevertheless operated under a climate of distrust and under a leadership that held strong racist views. Moreover, the division was severely constrained by manpower capabilities and afflicted by internal malaise and unsound leadership. There is no denying that the division's senior white officers held deeply prejudiced views of blacks, that they were conducting an experiment, and that they anticipated failure. Such a situation gave rise to a climate that was both stifling and devastating to blacks, and they helped to explain many of their failed combat operations. However, there were occasions when individual blacks rose to the challenge and demonstrated such stupendous feats of valor that even General Almond was forced to acknowledge them. Two such black soldiers were Second Lieutenant Vernon Baker and First Lieutenant John Fox. We shall take up their incredible story in the following chapters.

3

FROM CINQUALE TO HILL X AND MASSA

The fall of Massa, a heavily defended German stronghold in Italy, marked a decisive turning point of the war in the Mediterranean Theater of Operations. Previous attempts by the 92nd Infantry Division to seize and hold this city and its surrounding high grounds had ended in disaster. Beaten back time and again by the defending Germans, Massa proved an elusive target for the advancing troops. Its fall, however, in early spring of 1945, would set in motion a train of compelling events that would finally lead to American victory in Italy. Massa would demonstrate the appropriateness of effective planning and test the wisdom of allowing different racial elements in troop composition to work together toward the same objective. This operation, carried out after a series of earlier disasters, vindicated the view long held by blacks that troop integration particularly on the battlefield could lead to spectacular successes.

The Setting

After the abortive and disastrous attempts to cross the Cinquale Canal and efforts to dislodge the enemy in the Serchio Valley failed, the 92nd Division returned to the life of the "quiet sector"—a life of patrolling and training, passes and showers, movies and doughnut stands. The troops, severely jolted by these recent setbacks and searingly traumatic experiences, settled down to the not too unpleasant task of defending against an enemy who, himself, was reluctant to attack. The Germans for the most part were contented in their defensive role. During the second half of February and all of March 1945, the front line was just about the same as the one that appeared on the division's situation map in October 1944. And apart from some minor changes here and there, the same foxholes were being used, the same dugouts, the same gun positions, the same observation posts, and the same paths and approaches.

A 92nd Division infantryman, looking out from his frontline foxhole, beheld the same familiar sights. Up the coastal plain, the same ugly stretch of flatland extending right up to the cluster of trees and smokestacks and rooftops at the long sought objective of Massa greeted the eye. Curving across the flat marshland was the same Cinquale Canal, a constant reminder of their crushing defeat in February. It was here that the Germans unleashed their firepower with deadly accuracy and ferocity, resulting in many deaths, massive injuries, and the complete disarray of the advancing forces. On that eventful day the estuary of the canal ran red with American blood. And it was here that General Almond's ability as a military commander and strategist was put to the acid test. In the eyes of that infantryman and his fellow comrades and junior officers, Almond failed miserably on all counts.

Here also was Highway 1, still under enemy control, and far to the left the low hills of Punta Bianca, home of the Germans' giant coastal guns. Shells fired from these heavily defended and well-concealed guns exacted a heavy toll on the Division's movements, slowing their advance to a crawl. And off to the right were the same foothills of the Apennines. Rising high above them were the towering mountains, garrisoned by an entrenched enemy: Mount Ceretta, Mount Folgorito, Mount Carchio, Mount Altissimo, and other black peaks behind them, all of them hideous and formidable mountain masses, spotted with shrubs, but otherwise barren of natural vegetation. Across these desolate mountains were the same crags, and the same trails and gulches. And in the Serchio sector, the same river twisted in its snakelike course down the valley. If boredom had struck the 92nd Division soldier, that was but one of the prices he paid for failure in earlier efforts to push the line forward to more distant views and new scenery.

All across the Italian peninsula the line remained relatively the same. At the end of March, IV Corps, with its left flank on the Ligurian coast, held nearly 70 miles of Fifth Army's line. From left to right, its forces were lined up as follows: 92nd Infantry Division, 365th Infantry (detached), 1st Brazilian Division, 10th Mountain Division, and 81st Cavalry Reconnaissance Squadron of the 1st Armored Division. On IV Corps' right, east of the Reno River, the remaining twenty-five miles of the Army front was held by II Corps, with its 1st Armored Division and the 34th and 91st Infantry Divisions. Adjoining II Corps' right flank was the British 13th Corps.

From all indications, it appeared that the Germans were showing no intention of giving up Northern Italy without putting up a fierce struggle. At the end of winter, they still had twenty-three divisions there — some of the best in the Wehrmacht. In addition, they also had a number of Italian units, the equivalent of six Fascist divisions, and since the winter had brought only light casualties, they were able to bring most of their units up to strength. Forward ammunition supply dumps were also well stocked owing to the lightness of action during the winter stalemate. But if the Germans found their frontline situation satisfactory, conditions in the rear were getting worse due to constant bombing by Allied planes. Industrial and manufacturing facilities sustained devastating blows by air attacks; some of these plants were quickly salvaged and moved underground into natural and artificial caves, but their outputs fell drastically.

The enemy's transportation system was also deteriorating rapidly. Vehicle shortages were critically low, and the railroads, which could have brought in re-supply of these items, were under daily interdiction of Allied bombers. Trains were slowed down to a cautious, creeping gait, or as in numerous instances they waited for hours and even days for the signal to proceed. Tracks were under constant repair all along the lines of Northern Italy. Italian industry could offer little help since its badly damaged factories were unable to produce new trucks in sufficient quantities to offset the losses. With a severe shortage in the number of usable motor vehicles and with the gasoline supply line reduced to a mere trickle, enemy logistical planners were forced to turn to the horse and wagon and the ox-drawn cart. Numerous military vehicles were animal-drawn, with their engines turned on only on steep grades in the road. And to add to their woes, the Germans now faced a group of Italian partisans who were becoming increasingly bolder. American intelligence estimated that at least 50,000 Italians were ready to spring into action at the given signal. The constant threat of sabotage and guerrilla activity by the partisans forced the Germans to keep thousands of troops in the rear to guard their installations.

Allied Plans for the Spring Offensive

Against this weakened enemy situation, 15th Army Corps embarked on a bold and ambitious plan that called for the total destruction of the Germans in Italy. Allied commanders and planners were convinced that the time was propitious for such a course of action given the overall situation. Refilled, rested, and re-supplied, its divisions were poised for an all-out offensive aimed at the seizure of Verona and the containment of the enemy's main outlet from Italy. Part of the plan also envisioned that German resistance in western Italy would collapse of its own weight once the drive straight north of the Bologna-Verona axis commenced.

D-Day, set for April 10, 1945, and later brought forward by one day, would find the British Eighth Army making preliminary attacks on the Adriatic coast a few days before the American Fifth Army—the main effort of 15th Army Group—launched its own attack. The plan for Fifth Army's offensive, designated "Operation Craftsman," called for IV and II Corps to attack astride Highway 64 toward Bologna.

Operating under Fifth Army control and independent of IV Corps, the 92nd Infantry Division was slated to enter the fray on April 5 in a limited objective attack on the enemy's right flank against Massa. Allied planners trusted that this drive, scheduled for completion within five days, would force the enemy to commit his local reserves in their defense. In any event, the attack was expected to engage most, if not all, of the German 148th Grenadier Division, thereby preventing a diversion of any of its units to other fronts. To strengthen the 92nd for this crucial offensive operation, a general reorganization of the infantry elements of the division was undertaken with dispatch (refer to chapter 2 for details on reorganization).

In planning the April attack the defensive strength of the coastal plain was carefully considered. As the only flat, open approach to the north, it had become the most heavily defended part of the enemy's line. Minefields were thickly planted across the low, marshy plain, and the fields of fire extended for thousands of yards. Anti-tank obstacles dominated the approach, with the Cinquale Canal itself a natural and formidable barrier to tanks. Beyond the Cinquale there were four other tank barriers that cut across the open and expansive Ligurian plain. Each of these had prepared defenses. And they were, in the order in which the division would confront them, the Frigido River, Carrione Creek, the Parmignola River, and the Marga River. These four fortified water lines, sometimes referred to as the "Green Line Defense," gave the enemy a succession of natural defenses stretching miles in depth. All told, the Germans had done a masterful job in both their preparation and exploitation of natural barriers to defense.

General Almond dismissed the idea of attacking across the flat plains because of the enemy's strength in this area, and because of the division's earlier defeats here. Instead, he planned to push two regiments through the hills and mountains overlooking the plain. This tactic would also give considerable protection to the attacking regiments from the fire of the big coastal guns at Punta Bianca. The 442nd Japanese-American Regiment would move into line on the right of the 370th Infantry, strike through the mountains, bypass Massa, and seize Mount Brugiana due north of that city. In the meantime, the 370th, waiting in the lower hills, would push through to Montignoso, branch off to the sea north of the Cinquale Canal, and then turn to the north and drive on to the Frigidio River. The 371st, after being passed through by the 442nd and 370th regiments, would remain temporarily in its position. The 473rd in the Serchio Valley sector (except for its 2nd Battalion that would be kept in Division reserve) would hold its position "at all cost," conduct aggressive patrolling, and follow any enemy withdrawal without delay.

In official briefings conducted on February 26 General Almond pointed out that the new plan, Operation "Fourth Term," differed very little from the earlier plan, "Second Wind," which the division attempted to execute during the first few days of that month. He observed that Operation Fourth Term's "prospects of success are considered more favorable due to the substitution of troops of more combat reliability in the main effort, and by the assignment of the reorganized 370th Infantry to a role on the flat ground for which it is trained and psychologically better suited.... Variations in the plan from 'Fourth Term' are made to confuse the enemy as to our intentions. Diversionary efforts with this in view will supplement these operations. The enemy's reactions to 'Fourth Term,' as determined by radio intercepts and PW [prisoner of war] statements, indicate that excellent possibilities for success existed on 8, 9, and 10 February had the offensive power of the attack units been that expected of average infantry troops."[1]

The weeks immediately preceding the attack were marked by rising Allied activities in the rear areas, a noticeable contrast to the general quiet along the front. New artillery units were moved into the area to supplement the fire power of the division's organic artillery—the 329th and the 530th field artillery battalions, the British 76th Heavy Anti-Aircraft Regiment, a battery of the British 766th Anti-Aircraft Regiment, and A Company of the 84th Chemical Mortar Battalion.

Additional armor had also arrived as attachments—the 785th Light Tank Battalion and the 760th Tank Battalion (less two companies), the 679th and the 894th tank destroyer battalions. Artillery fires were to be concentrated in support of the main effort of the 442nd Infantry along the ridge since no direct attack was planned for the Serchio Valley. However, to confuse the enemy as to place and time of attack and to throw him off guard, a number of softening up TOTs (tests on targets) as simulated preparations was set for three days immediately preceding the main attack. The actual artillery bombardment on D-Day was to be short and intense. Air strikes by medium and heavy bombers were planned for the neutralization of the German heavy guns at Punta Bianca, and naval support using one battleship, two cruisers, and three destroyers was also requested.

Along with these reinforcing units, spring also arrived in the division combat area, a sharp contrast to the tired and physically demanding business of war. The olive trees on the top of Porta Ridge were green once again, and they waved their half-laden branches in the crisp yet melancholy air of the impending attack. Farmers, out in their fields once more, could see the hulking forms of tank destroyers hiding back in the shade where they awaited the order to unleash their fire power. And underneath the trees of Highway 1, huge piles of crated ammunition flanked the road for miles. Though warmer now, the back roads and trails were still soft with mud.

The Serchio, the Serra, and the Frigido rivers were rising and swelling their banks, and all the mountain streams, coming awake after the long winter, were rushing through the hills. Life had returned to valley and the mountaintops. There were unmistakable signs of new life and vibrancy everywhere and expectation filled the air. For the 92nd Infantry Division it was particularly noticeable in the myriad of activities undertaken. And for 2nd Lieutenant Vernon Baker, the attack on Hill X would become the grandstand for a display of bravery and courage under enemy fire heretofore not seen in this theater of operations.

The Opposing Forces, Approach, and Preparation

The enemy opposing the 92nd Division was still the 148th Grenadier Division. Behind its main defensive line were a number of local reserves—the Kesserlring Machine Gun Battalion, the 4th Mountain Battalion, elements of the Sam Marco Division, Monte Rosa Division, 285th Regiment, 135th Fortress Brigade, and a collection of German sailors and marines. And resting in the vicinity of Bologna, but ready for commitment at a moment's notice, was the 90th Panzer Grenadier Division.

While there had been no major changes in German dispositions since the ill-fated February attack, prisoners in Allied captivity were now reporting that the 148th Division was weeding out its Polish and

Italian troops—a move obviously designed to increase the combat reliability of its fighting units. The Germans were probably engaged in a similar exercise that General Almond undertook when he completely reorganized the 92nd Infantry Division, making it stronger and at the same time less black in its overall composition. With the jettisoning of Polish and Italian elements in the German lineup, the 92nd Division could therefore expect an even more determined enemy in the planned April attack. On the whole, the morale of the Germans on the 92nd Division's front was fairly high despite the disheartening news from the Fatherland and the grave situation they were experiencing in Italy.

At the start of April 1945, units of the 92nd Division line were disposed in the following manner: 370th Zone — 2nd Battalion (371st) from the Ligurian coast to Highway 1, 1st Battalion (370th) from Highway 1 to Mount Castiglione; 371st Zone — 3rd Battalion (371st) east to Seravazza, 2nd Battalion (371st) from Seravazza east for four miles across the mountains to the 473rd's boundary; 473rd Zone — 92nd Division Reconnaissance Troop and the 473rd Anti-Tank Company, with strong points, and lateral patrols east for three miles, then continuing eastward for another nine miles the 3rd Battalion of the 473rd Infantry Regiment. Finally, beyond the division's right boundary was the detached 365th Infantry, one of the original black regiments of the 92nd Division.

On the night of April 3–4, troops began their forward movement to await H-Hour. The 370th's 3rd Battalion, after its relief by the 371st's 2nd Battalion on the coastal plain, went back to an assembly area in order to get ready for the morning's attack. In the meantime, 1st Battalion of the 370th (which was to spearhead the regiment's attack) was relieved in position east of Highway 1 by the 3rd Battalion troops of the 371st the night before the attack commenced.

Nothing of significance occurred during the hours of darkness to betray the attack or to indicate that the enemy was alerted. However, during the late evening hours of April 4 the enemy began to lay smoke on the coastal flats, and by nightfall Hill X was under heavy bombardment. Shells also landed in the vicinity of Observation Post No. 1, at the Division's Command Post, and over on the flats west of Highway 1. An enemy combat patrol of an estimated eighteen men was discovered near the Division's forward lines but was quickly driven off in a short and swift shootout that resulted in zero casualties to American troops. Apart from this minor incident the outposts had little to report — at 0110 hours a white flare near the Cinquale Canal; at 0308 hours enemy fire falling near Strettoia; and at 0402 hours a white flare behind Hills X and Y.

The 1st Battalion of the 370th Regiment was reported in position at 0453 hours with A and C companies at their line of departure in the low hills east of Highway 1. Over to the right, 442nd's 100th Battalion was poised on Mount Cauala, ready to go. Its 3rd Battalion was plodding up the side of Mount Folgorito, thirty minutes behind schedule. Mortars and howitzers were ready, machine guns were laid and half-loaded, packs were on, and bandoleers were slung. Anxiously the men waited for their artillery preparation. Luminous dial watches slowly ticked off the last minutes. It was quiet. Breathing became heavier as H-Minute approached. The air was thick with expectancy. Now and then a rifle shot, a burp gun, or a mortar firing far away pierced the early morning silence. It was a clear night. There were stars in the sky, and out in front, rising up in frightful silhouette were the enemy's hills, and his mountains—steep, dark, and deadly, which the men of the 92nd Division had been ordered to capture.

At 0455 hours the anxiously awaited attack commenced. From far back in the rear came the booming of howitzers; shells came crashing down all across the front, lighting up the hills and ridges and the coastal plain. Closer up came the whum-ping of mortars and then more flashing light and shadows on the enemy ground. Machine guns of the 371st dug in along the front line joined in with a noisy staccato hammering, sending flaming bands of red tracers across the sky, while tank and tank destroyers in position near Highway 1 thundered in their contribution to the violent preparation. In the rear the sky over Querceta and Pietrasanta was a quivering pink, a flashing and flaring accompaniment to the low distant booming of guns. Light artillery and mortars concentrated on the known and suspected enemy batteries, emplacements, and strong points. The attack got underway at exactly 0500 hours on April 5, 1945, and it was a spectacular sight to behold.

Attack of the 370th Infantry Regiment

The first objective of the 370th was the Strettoia Hills. These hills rose out of the Strettoia hill mass, and for convenience in planning they had been designated Hills X, Y, and Z by the G-3 section. Hill X, the nearest of the three to the line of departure, rose in a series of terraces to a height of approximately 450 feet. North of Hill X was a shallow saddle beyond which stood Hill Y (600 feet), which extended north until it was cut by the east-west Montignoso draw. East of Hill Y, and separated from it by only a shallow draw, was Hill Z, with an elevation of 600 feet also. The attack plan called for the 1st and 3rd Battalions to strike northwest, while the 2nd Battalion, moving up behind the 1st, would descend into the coastal plain when it had reached the Porta Ridge just before the famed Castle Aghinolfi.

The First Day

With companies A and C moving abreast, 1st Battalion would commence its attack at 0500 hours against Hill X. The 3rd Battalion, following to the right rear one hour later was to capture and hold Strettoia. The advance of the regiment was then to continue to the north to the high ground overlooking Montignoso. Moving out promptly with the artillery preparation at 5 o'clock that morning, A Company advanced rapidly up Hill X from the south, while C Company was hitting it from the west. By dawn A Company had moved on to occupy Hill X, having encountered little enemy resistance and having bypassed many enemy soldiers on their way. But suddenly the entrenched Germans, awakened and alert, struck back. A fierce firefight broke out and as casualties mounted, disorganization set in rapidly. Many of the men began to "melt away." Attempts by A Company to recapture the hill and hold their position ended in failure.

However, the story with C Company was somewhat different. Its advance was so rapid that in the first two hours it had reached a point nearly 3,000 yards behind the enemy's most forward positions and was east of the towering and resplendent Castle Aghinolfi, the strongly defended enemy observation post. At 0455 hours C Company, less its 1st Platoon, which was scheduled to attack up the west side of Hill X, moved out on the run across the level ground before the Strettoia hill mass, taking advantage of the artillery preparation. Before the fires had lifted it had moved up to a point approximately 100 yards from enemy positions in the foothills. The men now waited here along the banks of a muddy canal while a hastily formed detail cleared a path through a mined area. Soon they were climbing the steep rocky grade to Point Baker, the first objective on the Porta Ridge. An American force was finally on the ridge, much to the dismay of the Germans. Alerted to this new development, the enemy immediately cranked up their heavy mortars and brought down concentrated fire on the company. Some of the men hastily took cover in a draw where anti-personnel mines inflicted even more casualties.

Continuous and accurate enemy fire and the subsequent disorganization of the troops combined to reduce the company's strength to twenty-five men and four officers. However, the company re-grouped and continued to advance along the Porta Ridge to a point 250 yards from Castle Aghinolfi, the battalion's major objective. Moving swiftly, the troops actually ran forward, stopping only to catch their breath or to cut communication wires. During this phase of rapid advance only two casualties were sustained. Captain John Runyon, C Company's white commander, recalled very vividly this phase of the attack:

> During the melee I was separated from my radio operator, who carried both the 300 set and my 536 set. I kept close contact with the artillery observer, 2d Lt. Walker, and as fast as possible called for artillery fires to precede our advance toward the castle and the battalion objective. Practically every time we called for fires it would be necessary to repeat coordinates over and over again, mainly because some party on the receiving end did not believe our coordinates to be correct or that we had advanced as far and as fast as we reported. However, when the fire orders were acknowledged we had excellent support, and it is a credit to the Artillery, Lt. Walker, and to the men of C Company that we followed our artillery fire as close as 100 yards at times with no casualties suffered. More than a dozen communication wires were cut and this factor alone, I believe, saved the lives of quite a few of us later on.[2]

Meanwhile, Second Lieutenant Vernon Baker, assigned to C Company, advanced at the head of his weapon's platoon. Moving more rapidly than the rest of C Company, Lieutenant Baker and about twenty-five men within two hours reached the south side of a draw some 250 yards from Castle Aghinolfi. In reconnoitering for a suitable position to set up a machine gun, Baker observed two cylindrical objects jutting out of a slit in a mount at the edge of a hill. Crawling up the hill and under the mount's opening, he quickly stuck his M-1 rifle into the slit and emptied the clip, killing the observation post's two occupants. Dashing off to another position in the same area, he stumbled upon a well-camouflaged machine gun nest, the crew of which was having breakfast. Before they could scramble their weapons Baker shot and killed both machine gunners.[3]

With a lull in enemy mortar fire, Captain Runyon summoned Lieutenant Baker for a quick conference to strategize on reinforcements and withdrawal. At this point C Company had suffered several dead and dozens wounded. During this tête-à-tête, a German soldier appeared from the draw and hurled a grenade at them. The flying missile, a wooden handled potato masher grenade, dropped near Captain Runyon's feet but failed to explode. The conversation ended abruptly. Runyon scrambled for and sought cover in an abandoned house nearby. Lieutenant Baker, on the other hand, instinctively turned and faced the direction from which the grenade had come. Catching a glimpse of the fleeing enemy soldier, Baker dashed off in hot pursuit. As the enemy tried to make it into the sanctuary of his dugout, Baker shot him twice in the back before he buckled and hit the ground. Accurate shot that he was and mustering tremendous courage, Baker went down into the draw alone. An eerie feeling it was. Appearing before him was a strange looking object, one that he felt compelled to investigate. It was a dugout. Without a moment's hesitation he blasted open the concealed entrance of this dugout with a grenade, shot one German soldier who emerged after the explosion, tossed another grenade into the dugout and entered, firing his Thompson submachine gun, killing two more Germans.

As Lieutenant Baker climbed back out of the draw, enemy machine gun and mortar fire began to inflict heavy casualties on the little platoon of twenty-five, killing or wounding two-thirds of them. Baker made his way out safely and went in search of Captain Runyon. Finding Runyon taking cover in an old abandoned house, Baker informed him of what transpired, and noted during an interview with the author that the captain was visibly shaken and terrified. After this episode, the two reports by Baker and Runyon of what happened afterward differed substantially. According to Baker, Runyon left to go down the hill, promising to return with reinforcements. Baker and his wounded men remained in their location until dusk, before withdrawing to Battalion headquarters down the hill. The captain never returned. Runyon, on the other hand, reported a different story:

> Feeling definitely responsible to the wounded who had given their best efforts, I ordered that a withdrawal be made in two groups. I knew it was a big disappointment to many to have to withdraw, but we were too small to hold out any longer in that exposed position.... Lieutenant Baker broke down into tears. "Captain," he said, "we can't withdraw. We must stay here and fight it out." I knew Lieutenant Baker desperately wanted these men of "C" Company to hold their ground and that he was willing to sacrifice his own life in an effort to win our battle.[4]

Continuing his report, Runyon said, "As I recall, I told him [Baker] that I was perfectly willing to stay there with him and fight it out; but that as long as our men persisted in bunching up so that each time a mortar shell landed in our area we suffered two and three casualties, we didn't have a chance. I told him if he could get the men to separate and 'dig in' we would stay there. Lieutenant Baker and I made one last effort to place our men in a defensive position. But again we failed. I sincerely believe that our failure was largely due to the fact that many of these boys were strangers to one another and had never served together before in active combat. Furthermore, at this stage of the fight several of our noncommissioned officers had already become casualties and we were without their services.

"Lieutenant Baker, who had throughout the day displayed magnificent courage, volunteered to cover the withdrawal of the first group which consisted of quite a few walking wounded. There were also wounded cases in the second group. Both parties successfully withdrew by different routes. Both parties encountered enemy machine gun positions, which approaching from the rear they were able to knock out. More communication wires were cut. During the withdrawal, four different enemy machine gun crews were destroyed without loss to our group. In all cases the enemy were taken by complete surprise and were unable to effectively use their weapons against us."⁵

Baker on the other hand gave a different account. In a taped interview at his home in Idaho in August 1996, Baker reiterated the same account he gave in a report submitted to General Almond in June 1945. When the late Colonel John Cash and the author interviewed him in April 1994 while researching his story for the Medal of Honor project, Baker also told the same story, steadfastly maintaining the point that Captain Runyon left for reinforcements and never returned. Baker's told the author in 1996: "I had six men plus my platoon sergeant and myself. Total of eight men. We couldn't move; there was no moving. I decided we would go back. No orders from nobody. Captain Runyon had been gone about three hours. No reinforcements. No re-supply. Our artillery had stopped; we had no observer, no radio. We turned our backs on in and moved out; I was leading the way. No rear guard; just eight men in a group on skirmish line headed back home, down the same direction we came up. Found two machine gun bunkers that we had missed on the way up. Got fire from them and put down one of my men. Sgt. Thomas found himself a BAR [Browning automatic rifle] and as we were going along, got fire from machine guns, he put down suppressing fire with BAR. He had the classic BAR assault position. I crawled toward him and he fired over my head. It was close and I was hoping like hell he didn't have a wild round. He held them down 'til I got to them and used grenades to take them out. No more small arms fire from there, but we did get it from hills to our left and mortar fire. They followed us all the way back to the tree line on slopes of Hill X. Had couple men got scratches from tree bursts.

"We took a different route to the bottom; instead of rear slope we went straight down to highway. Got down to highway and told rest of men to go back to Company CP. I sat down and puked my guts out right there on the highway. After that I got up and headed back to Company CP. First sergeant and company clerk were there. First sergeant called Battalion and told them that I was back with what was left of the men. I was summoned to the battalion and told to report to Lieutenant Colonel Murphy, the commander. He'd been running the 1st Battalion 370th for about six months. Reported to him while he was sitting in the middle of the room in a bathtub. I walked in, reported in, told me don't worry about saluting just sit down. He said, 'I understand you had it pretty rough up the hill.' Runyon had already talked to him. But he didn't tell me that Captain Runyon's opinion was that we would not be coming back. Runyon thought that we were done for; I found that out from the Battalion S3 after the war was over. I didn't see Runyon there. I told Murphy what had happened up there. He said it seemed like we had done a good job. Told me go back to my company and get some rest."[6]

Thus on April 5, 1945, the men of C Company had killed twenty-six Germans, wounded many others, and destroyed six machine gun positions, two observer posts, and four dugouts. Baker himself had accounted for nine of the dead enemy soldiers, three of the machine gun nests, an observer post, and a dugout. The position above the draw in front of the castle, however, was the high tide, not only of C Company's advance but also that of the 370th Infantry Regiment. In fact, the major elements of the regiment never really got going during the first two days of the offensive.

In the meantime — at 0745 hours that morning — B Company, back in its reserve position near the line of departure, was ordered to move up to Hill X and reinforce A Company. But this comparatively easy assignment — to place reinforcements on an already occupied hill — turned out to be extremely difficult for the battalion. Company officers were unable to get their men moving, and additional leadership had to be supplied by the battalion commanders and staff. By 1045 hours, forty-five men of B Company finally made it to the hill, the rest drifted away. With these men and the remnants of A Company, Colonel Murphy began to organize a defensive position. During this phase of the morning's operation, both friendly and enemy smoke had obscured air and ground observation, but artillery fires continued.

The attack of the 3rd Battalion operating to the right of the regimental area met with even less success than that of the 1st Battalion. At 0600 hours, while preparation fires were falling on Strettoia and the rocky ridge leading to Hill Z, the battalion was hit by heavy enemy mortar concentrations. The situation at the close of the first day was: 1st Battalion occupying Hill X; 2nd Battalion occupying Hill Y; and 3rd Battalion reorganizing where it had disintegrated that morning. Casualties on this first day amounted to four officers and ten enlisted men killed; five officers and 109 enlisted men wounded; and fifteen enlisted men missing. And despite the frequent disorganization and "melting away" of several units of the 370th this day, only one member of the regiment was apprehended by the division's straggler line where MPs collected men who wandered into the rear areas.

The Second Day

The plan of attack for the second day called for the 2nd Battalion to move out from hills X and Y at 0600 hours and seize Castle Aghinolfi and the high ground overlooking the Montignoso draw, where Captain Runyon and Lieutenant Baker had been the previous day. The 1st Battalion would reorganize and be prepared to pass through the 2nd Battalion, while the 3rd Battalion would be ready to move on call to occupy the flatland north of the Cinquale Canal.

At 0555 hours, five minutes before the troops were to move out from their designated location, the artillery began its preparation fires on enemy positions. Not to be outdone, the Germans countered by placing heavy concentrations of their own on hills X and Y where the 2nd Battalion was nervously waiting at the line of departure. The effect was devastating. Pandemonium broke loose and disorganization among the rank and file quickly ensued, causing the attack to be postponed until 0800 hours. The enemy had intercepted radio messages about the impending attack, and they were ready and waiting for the precise moment to unleash their firepower on hills X and Y. Efforts to commence the attack at 0800 hours failed again because of enemy fire and internal disorganization within the 2nd Battalion. One hour later, the battalion was still pinned down with fresh barrages of enemy mortar fire. Men began drifting down the hillsides away from this fire, and the battalion became utterly disorganized and scattered. The 2nd Battalion's contribution to the attack that day was zero.

The 1st Battalion, in position on Hill X, was ordered at 1330 hours to seize and occupy a designated spot on the Porta Ridge. But before the attack commenced, Captain Donald Counts, the commander of E Company, was fatally shot in the chest while running across an open space to get into the attack position. Disorganization immediately set in as men fled in different directions seeking cover and safety. One and a half hours later and after persistent efforts to reorganize the troops, the battalion commander reported to regimental headquarters that he was experiencing great difficulty getting the men into line for the attack. Repeated efforts failed to get the troops to advance, despite supporting fires.

By 1830 hours as evening approached, the battalion had whittled down to eighty-three riflemen; the rest had slowly melted away and unaccounted for. With a confused and bewildering situation that seemed beyond redemption that day, the 1st Battalion was ordered to organize a defensive line with the men it had, and hold it for the night. In the morning the 2nd Battalion of the 473rd Infantry Regiment would take over the battalion's mission. At the end of the second day, the 1st Battalion was now on the left of Hill Y, but still far short of its objective — Montignoso; the 2nd Battalion, on the right of Hill Y, gained no ground; and the 3rd Battalion, which had been relieved of its mission to capture Strettoia, was in division reserve in the vicinity of Pozzi.

Because of repeated failures during the past two days of the battalions of the 370th to advance despite supporting fires, General Almond decided to switch the regimental areas of the 370th and the 473rd. The latter, a white attached regiment, whose troops he considered better suited for the attack, would come over to the coastal sector and undertake the offensive mission of the 370th Infantry Regiment. This change came into effect on the third day of the attack. Meanwhile, the 370th would be assigned to patrolling duties in the relatively quiet Serchio Valley sector.

The Third Day

At 0500 hours on April 7, the 473rd's 2nd Battalion, having been brought up from division reserve the previous night, moved out along the Porta Ridge. Two hours later all three companies were on the ridge, and by 0900 hours they had reached a line running generally east from Porta to Hill Y. Captain Runyon and Lieutenant Vernon Baker, having traversed this terrain two days earlier, were ordered to lead the battalion up the trail. Recalling this part of the saga, Baker said, "That night I was told to report to the regimental commander — bring yourself and your platoon sergeant back to regiment. Colonel Sherman told me, 'you are going to take a unit of the 473rd Infantry same route you went up yesterday, and show them where to go.' A white infantry unit! Which I did. My platoon sergeant went with one company, I went with another company. One of the officers from B Company took another unit up. We walked up on the hill and up to the Castle [Aghinolfi]." Although heavy enemy fire was encountered the battalion continued to advance throughout the day. By evening F Company, the most forward element of the battalion, had pushed along the ridge almost to the castle. At the close of the third day, the 2nd Battalion of the 473rd, held up by artillery fire, remained on the Porta Ridge, with F Company outposting positions near Castle Aghinolfi.

Enemy Withdrawal

Sunday morning, the fourth day, was ominously silent — a quiet, eerie feeling blanketed the atmosphere. No enemy artillery or mortar shells could be heard, there was not even the sound of small arms fire. It was obvious that the Germans had broken off contact during the night and hastily withdrawn. Patrols of the 370th's 3rd Battalion moved through Porta Ridge, and finding it undefended, continued without opposition to the junction of Highway 1 and the Montignoso draw. The enemy was definitely withdrawing and according to Baker, Germans "were falling back." But despite slight rear guard resistance, the advances in the regimental sector during the day were very slow. By 1800 hours troops had reached no further than the south bank of the Margo River. The 473rd's 2nd Battalion occupied Montignoso and other towns in the draw, and made contact with the Japanese-American 442nd Infantry Regiment on the right flank.

That night troops of the 473rd's 1st Battalion, newly arrived from the Serchio Valley, shuffled up Highway 1 in the dark, escorted by tanks of the 760th Tank Battalion. This fresh force had the mission of driving quickly into Massa and occupying it. However, tank traps, mines, heavy artillery and mortar fire, and strong rear guard resistance blunted its rapid advance. As a result the column was forced to halt at some point and deploy its forces. Fighting continued on the outskirts of Massa throughout April 9. B Company, the most forward element of the 473rd, was about a quarter of a mile short of the center of the city.

The 2nd Battalion advanced across fields and groves and was able to come on line with the 1st Battalion by evening. During the night both battalions sent out strong patrols into the city. The 370th's 3rd Battalion straggled badly during the day before being relieved by E Company and a machine gun platoon of the 2nd Battalion. The rest of the 370th's 2nd Battalion remained in the coastal area with the mission of guarding the 473rd's right flank.

Protected by a cordon of mountains to the east, the enemy continued to defend Massa well into Monday, April 9. But tanks of the 758th and 760th Tank Battalions, after fighting all day against machine gun nests and snipers, reached the center of the city and resistance collapsed. Early in the morning of April 10, B Company of the 473rd Infantry advanced into Massa without encountering any fierce enemy opposition. By 0800 hours, Italian partisans struck from the hills in record numbers. But fanatic German rear guard troops covering the retreat of their fleeing comrades swiftly reacted by delivering concentrated machine gun and mortar fire across the river. However, quick action by the 442nd Infantry Regiment had cut off almost all avenues of escape for the fleeing Germans. That regiment, commencing its attack on April 5, advanced rapidly in the mountains and after four days had reached the heights overlooking Massa from the east. Their envelopment action, fast, bold, and yet magnificent, was one of the outstanding performances during the entire Italian campaign.

Triumph at Last

The entry into Massa was like a triumphant march. Italian partisans armed with machine guns and pistols swarmed the streets of the city that was once famous for its marble works and sculpture. Less than two-thirds of Massa's population had remained in the city when it fell into Allied hands. Women and children greeted American soldiers with bouquets of roses, lilacs, and lilies. Lieutenant Baker recalled this moment of jubilation: "We were walking through villages to accolades and flowers. One particular village lady came out and she looked at me, saw my bars, grabbed me and shouted 'Teniente! Teniente!' You want signorigna? She had a house full of them. We said no thanks."[7] By midday, the city was in a festive mood as huge crowds gathered in the center of the town to celebrate victory. Two days later on Wednesday, April 11, troops began to pour into Massa. It became the first major Italian objective to fall into Allied hands in the spring offensive. The fall of Massa opened a gaping wound in German defenses and finally led to their ultimate defeat in Italy. The offensive against this well fortified and heavily defended German stronghold also marked a decisive turning point in the history of the 92nd Infantry Division. Flushed with victory, the division continued its relentless attack, sweeping 100 miles to the north and west until all enemy forces surrendered. After Massa came La Spezia and other important towns along the coast, and then finally Genoa on April 27, 1945. All told, the division overran nearly 3,000 square miles of Italian territory, mostly mountainous, rugged, and very treacherous.

As the war in Italy was finally coming to an end, Second Lieutenant Vernon Baker was about to be honored with the Army's second highest decoration for gallantry in combat — the Distinguished Service Cross. He would also linger a while longer in Italy, meeting and falling in love with a signorina.

4

VERNON BAKER:
A MEDAL, A SIGNORINA,
AND A NEW LIFE

On May 2, 1945, the war in Italy came to an end when Lieutenant General Heinrich Von Vietinghoff, commander in chief of the German Army Group Southwest, signed terms of unconditional surrender in Caserta. Before the week ended, an unconditional German surrender was signed in a "little red school house" in Rheims, France. World War II was finally over in Europe. The Allied Spring Offensive that began in Italy on April 5 and lasted twenty-eight days resulted in the capture of large quantities of enemy equipment and nearly 20,000 prisoners. The 92nd Infantry Division expended about five million rounds of all types of ammunition, totaling some 9,000 tons. But while victory was sweet and euphoric, it came at a price and did generate new responsibilities. Combat duties for the black soldiers of the division were now replaced with new duties and these added tasks triggered new problems—the terms of surrender had to be enforced, the enemy had to be disarmed and his movement closely guarded and controlled, and troops had to be re-deployed. Indeed, victory came with its own price tag, setting in motion its own dynamic.

But while these concerns were real and pressing at the time, they were overshadowed by the larger strategic imperative of the war in the Pacific. The War Department quickly established policies for the re-deployment of troops to the United States and the Pacific Command. On June 10, the 92nd Division, now comprising of its three original infantry regiments, began to leave Genoa by trucks to a concentration area south of the town of Viareggio.

Seven days later on June 17 the move was completed. Within a few days after the division arrived at its new location, an intensive training program began, aimed at preparing troops for re-deployment, with General Edward Almond designated by Fifth Army as commanding general of the Viareggio training area. He remained at this seaside resort town until his departure on August 12 for a new assignment in the United States as commanding general of the 2nd Infantry Division. Two days later Japan surrendered. All anxiety and concerns about deployment to the Pacific evaporated. World War II was over at last. American troops everywhere began preparing for the long journey home. For the black soldiers of the 92nd Division this day would come on November 16 when they set sail from the Italian Port of Livorno. But this would not be the case for Lieutenant Baker. He would stay in Italy for another eighteen months. This chapter explores four major aspects of his life — joining the U.S. Army, his receipt of the Distinguished Service Cross, his love affair with an Italian signorina during his sojourn in Italy, and his return to the United States and receipt of the Medal of Honor.

Joining the Army

Born on December 17, 1919, in Cheyenne, Wyoming, Vernon Baker was orphaned at an early age when both his parents died in an automobile accident in 1923. He grew up with his grandparents and attended several schools, finally graduating from high school in Clarinda, a farm town in rural Iowa. He returned to Cheyenne in 1939, a few months before his grandfather died in December.

The young high school graduate looked around for work and

eventually found a job at the Army post building new cantonment areas on the base. It was a night job, 8 p.m. to 3 a.m., picking up waste lumber and stacking it. Describing the routine of that job years later Baker said, "When we went to work a guy would stand up there, passing out job assignments, then he would say: 'Now, the names I call out will go over to the nigger barracks.' I got tired of hearing that word every night and quit after a week."[1]

His sister, Olivia, worried that Vernon might drift into trouble, urged him to look into joining the Army. In early April 1942, young Vernon and a buddy, Carl Green, walked into the Army Recruiting Station at Cheyenne. The sergeant behind the desk took one look at them and said: "There ain't no quota for you people right now." Vernon and his friend walked out, disgusted, and swore they'd never come back. But this was not for long.

Vernon Baker had sat around Cheyenne long enough and his sister was on his case. Two months after his first attempt to join the Army, he reluctantly returned on June 1 to the Army Recruiting Station downtown one more time, thinking as he went along that he had nothing to lose. On this occasion, however, a different sergeant sat behind the desk. He greeted Baker warmly and invited him to sit down. Surprised and somewhat excited, Baker took a seat and began filling out enlistment papers. The sergeant also told him to return on June 26 to go to Fort Warren for his physical examination and processing into the Army. Baker could hardly believe what he was hearing. He would leave from there to a basic training base. On the appointed day the sergeant drove him to the post and he was on his way.

The following day, June 27, they boarded a train to Fort Riley, Kansas, Baker and another black man drafted out of Laramie, Wyoming. At Fort Riley they drew uniforms and equipment and went through further processing steps on their way into the Army, the Green Machine. Then they boarded a train bound for Camp Walters, took seats and sat back for the long journey to Texas. Suddenly a porter appeared and told the two black recruits to follow him. They followed him to the rear, without question, until they reached a rail car with only black people occupying the seats. "Something clicked," Baker said. "We had crossed the line into Oklahoma." It was only the first taste of reality, Southern style.

In Mineral Wells, Texas, Baker got off the train and walked slowly to a bus for the ride to Camp Walters. He stepped in, put his bag on the front seat and sat down. There were only three other people on the bus, two whites and one elderly black man in the very back. The driver turned around and told the young soldier: "Nigger, get to the back of this bus where you belong." Baker's jaw tightened and with fists clinched he was getting ready to fight the sullen bus driver when he felt a tap on his shoulder. It was an old black man. "Son, come with me, I got something to explain to you," he said. On the back seat of that bus, a rural Southern black man explained the facts of segregation, the Jim Crow laws that legally relegated black people to inferior status and separated them from their white "betters," to a young Western black man: Everything is separate down here, where you ride on a train or bus, where you sleep, where you eat, which fountain you drink water from. Always step out of the way of white folks. Don't look at white women. Don't ever start no fight with a white man.

Pondering these words of the wise old man, Baker felt enraged and helpless. The rest of the journey was spent in quiet contemplation. He reminisced about his upbringing, the freedom of movement he was accustomed to back home, and how things have suddenly changed. It was as if he was entering a strange and vastly different world. While in this state of reverie, the bus came to a screeching halt, jolting him out of his slumber. The announcement of his stop sent him rushing to the door of the bus. In an instant Baker was out, forgetting to even say goodbye to the old man. At last, the gates of Camp Walters stood before him. He entered through its portals and walked into the reality of the segregated Army.

"We were off in one corner of the south end of camp, and we had our own little PX, our own mess hall, our own little clubs," Baker said. "There were more black people there than I'd ever seen in my life. One of the first people I met was Eli Brooks of Boys Town." There were more lessons to be learned about Army reality. On his first payday Baker drew $13. There was a crap game in the latrine and Vernon figured to make a killing. He lost every dime he had in his pocket. That was his welcome to Army life.

His military initiation was mostly standard basic boot camp — physical training, marching, and constantly getting yelled at. The training company officers were all white; the sergeants were all black — old line Regular Army sergeants and corporals who had served a long career in one or the other of the four all-black Army regiments Congress had created after the Civil War. They singled out the biggest and dumbest of the trainees, placed armbands on these men, and then put them in charge of the rest of the trainees. It was the Army's way of using old and tried hands to leaven the young and undisciplined.

Upon completion of basic training, Baker's platoon was assigned to Fort Huachuca, Arizona. The journey was long and tedious, traveling by train across some of the widest and emptiest expanses of Texas, New Mexico, and Arizona. In the middle of the night their cars were parked on a siding in the big middle of nowhere. Welcome to Fort Huachuca. Early the next morning the new arrivals were marched up a hill to the Old Post. A new cantonment had been built down below on the plains. After a night in the old barracks atop the hill a black sergeant had Baker's group fall out. He walked up and down the line, then asked, "Anybody here use a typewriter?" Baker recalled older soldiers talking about never volunteering for anything in the Army, but he and two other men stepped forward. The sergeant walked them down to the new post, a mile or so away, and made the rounds of three of the companies of the 25th Regiment, dropping off one new company clerk at each location. He walked Vernon Baker into the D Company orderly room and announced, "First Sergeant Allen, here's your new company clerk." It was October 1941. Baker would hold that job for about six months, encompassing the beginning of America's involvement in World War II.

The first sergeant informed him at the outset that many of the men in D Company couldn't read or write, were totally illiterate, and one of his jobs on payday would be to sign their names. Those men would mark an "X" on the payroll ledger and Baker, as company clerk, would write their names underneath. He performed this service for 30 to 35 percent of the men of Company D. "I didn't realize there were people in this country who couldn't read or write," Baker said, adding, "That got to me. These men resented us youngsters coming in with a little education. It created divisions within our ranks."

The brand-new company clerk watched as, one by one, the best black noncommissioned officers (NCOs) of the 25th Regiment were shipped off to Fort Benning, Georgia, to attend Officer Candidate School (OCS). A wave of new draftees, a fair share of them black, was beginning to wash over the tiny peacetime Army and black junior officers were needed in growing numbers. D Company's supply sergeant was one of those sent to Fort Benning, and the next thing Baker knew he was standing in front of the desk of Captain Green, the D Company commander. He announced, "You're my new supply sergeant; take over the supply room." Baker said, "I had typed all the forms, requisitions, inventory sheets, so I knew that supply room. I took it over." A month later the captain called him in again and handed him the three stripes of a buck sergeant. In less than a year Baker had gone from a private, drawing $21 a month, to a sergeant, drawing $60 a month, with his own private room at one end of a barracks.

In the outfit there were still many of the old soldiers, the cadre of that little section of a small Army reserved for blacks: PFCs, corporals and buck sergeants who had spent 20 years wearing the uniform, enduring the boredom and grind of military service, waiting six, eight or ten years just to earn another stripe. Because the black Army meant a steady job with a regular paycheck no one ever left voluntarily. Advancement was stagnated; someone had to retire or die before someone else obtained a promotion to a rank he may have earned, and deserved, for years. Baker recalled, "Some of these guys were mean. When us youngsters started coming in and becoming instant sergeants they resented it. Just after the war began, every rank in the unit was upgraded by one stripe, and I became a staff sergeant. I began to really have a hard time with those old Army Regulars. I couldn't get through to them."

One night in the spring of 1942, coming back to barracks from the post's movie theater, three of the old cadre sergeants of the regiment jumped on Sergeant Baker and beat the hell out of him. "They told me: you're one of those smart niggers, got them stripes. They whipped my ass good. I never forgot that and I never forgot them," Baker said. He didn't report the incident. "I kept it to myself, figuring I would get even."

Not long afterward Baker was summoned to regimental headquarters and found himself standing in front of the commander's desk. The colonel told him he was applying for Officer Candidate School.

4. Vernon Baker: A Medal, a Signorina, and a New Life

Said Baker: "I didn't particularly want to go to OCS. I had a good job and I was happy. But I was told: You WILL sign here." The application was filed, and the regiment was shipped to Spokane, Washington, to guard Geiger Field during those panicky months after Pearl Harbor when there were widespread fears that the Japanese would attack and invade the West Coast. In October 1942, as the regiment was returning home to Fort Huachuca, Staff Sergeant Baker got his orders to report to Fort Benning, Georgia, to attend Officer Candidate School.

At Fort Benning, Baker was assigned to an all-black platoon in a white training company, Class 148. He was one of fifty-two blacks in his platoon; over the next three months that number dwindled down through normal attrition to approximately twenty-five that finally graduated and were commissioned as officers, if not exactly gentlemen in the eyes of the white Army. In Baker's words the Army was "shoveling us through in huge numbers." An officer candidate in Baker's class summoned enough courage and asked an instructor why the Army was turning out so many new second lieutenants. His reply: "Because they are expendable." During his time at OCS, Baker said, there was no leave, no visits to town, no time off. The training officers and cadre were all white. He added that the blacks in the training company were treated fairly.

On January 11, 1943, Staff Sergeant Baker traded in his stripes for the shiny gold bars of a brand-new second lieutenant in the United States Army, and was sent right back to Fort Huachuca, to the newly re-designated 370th Infantry Regiment, Company C, as a rifle platoon leader. "I went along to the old Company, now called K," Baker remembers. "I called out every one of those three sergeants who had beat me up, locked their heels together, braced them at attention and ate them raw. I got my revenge, and it wasn't violent either."

Baker inherited a full strength rifle platoon. Black units typically were at 100 percent or more of authorized strength because there was nowhere else to send black draftees. At times the platoons and the company even had too many corporals and sergeants, because they had nowhere else to go. Lt. Baker's outfit was now a part of the recently formed 92nd Infantry Division, one of two all-black divisions being created in the United States. The other was the 93rd Infantry Division.

The atmosphere at Fort Huachuca had changed with the arrival of the 92nd Division. "When the 25th Regiment was there by itself, when the war started, we were fairly close and our morale on 7 December 1941 was all good," Baker said, adding, "The prevailing attitude was: let's go whip some ass." He returned to Huachuca only to find all sense of esprit and unit cohesion evaporated under the daily grind of monotonous training, the importance and purpose of which was never adequately explained by Division commanders. White officers came and went, rotating through brief stays in command of the black units and moving on to better jobs. The troops, according to Baker, just didn't give a damn.

The wave of black draftees that poured in to Huachuca was sullen and rebellious. "Most draftees came in with a bad attitude by reason of the way they were treated before they got into service, and when they got to the Army they brought that same attitude with them," Baker said. "The feeling was that we were never going into combat, that we were considered no good for combat."

Fort Huachuca is out in the middle of the Arizona desert, a particularly isolated outpost, and that is one reason the Army based black units there. There was no town of any size within easy reach and the Army thus avoided the frictions generated by having black soldiers on weekend passes in white communities. Huachuca and all the old Western forts and posts had known plenty of black troops and cavalrymen since shortly after the end of the Civil War. Congress decreed that the Army would always have four regiments of black soldiers but the Army decreed that those units would be kept out of sight and out of mind of white America by assigning them to the most remote regions of the wild West.

The isolation, and the lack of communication from higher headquarters, turned the place into a hotbed of rumors. One that started in early 1943 had the 92nd Division going into combat, probably in the Pacific Theater. It was dismissed out of hand by most black soldiers and officers; they didn't believe they would ever be used as anything more than service troops—cooks, truck drivers, stevedores, ditch diggers. That was the way it had been in the Army for the most part since World War I, and that was the way they expected it would remain. Optimism was near dead, overtaken by a plethora of false rumors and a preponderance of ignorance.

4. Vernon Baker: A Medal, a Signorina, and a New Life

Conventional wisdom was wrong this time. On a bright, sunny hot day in early June 1943, the division chief of staff called out all black officers to Division Headquarters up on the hill. They assembled under one of the large trees at the end of the old HQ building. The speech, as Baker remembers it, was galling. The message: There's a war being fought and white boys over there are getting killed; now it's time for the black boys to go over and get killed. This division is preparing to go into combat.

Now the word around camp was that the 370th Regiment would be beefed up and become the 370th Regimental Combat Team (RCT) and would be the first unit to go overseas into the fighting. A number of officers and NCOs pulled every string they could to get transferred out to the 370th's sister regiments, the 360th and 361st Regiments, in hopes of remaining in the States. It would avail them little; eventually the entire division ended up in Italy in combat. The 370th did a good deal of weeding out of its own: everyone who had physical or mental problems was transferred out and better men from the other regiments were transferred in to replace them.

The men of the 370th knew they were getting ready to go somewhere, but didn't know where. Orders came down to all units to turn in all uniforms, weapons, and field equipment. Those orders immediately ignited the rumor mill, setting a virtual firestorm of idle and baseless gossip that the new equipment that would replace infantry gear would be picks and shovels; that the 370th had been stripped of its weapons and now would become a road and bridge building unit. Those rumors, however, died a quick death with the arrival of crate after crate of brand-new uniforms, gear, and weapons. The officers drew new .30-caliber carbines; the enlisted men new M-1 Garand rifles; the heavy weapons platoons new Browning automatic rifles (BARs) and new machine guns.

Soon enough the 370th RCT, and Lieutenant Baker, were on their long journey to the battlefield, and it was toward the East Coast, not the West, toward the European Theater, not the Pacific. They moved by train to Newport News, Virginia, where the USS *Mariposa* waited for them. Short leaves were given prior to the sailing date, but Vernon Baker was too far from home to bother. "I stayed back and studied my field manuals," Baker recalled, adding, "I wasn't shipping over there to get my ass shot off. I was determined I was going to survive." That desire would bring Baker into closer contact with the men of his rifle platoon as the *Mariposa* sailed toward Europe. The twenty-two-year-old lieutenant spent as much time as possible below decks with his troops, talking and listening. He recalled, "We began to realize we were going into this thing together and if we didn't hang together we wouldn't survive. Then they understood, and that was a happy time for me on the voyage over. I began to enjoy knowing my black brothers. The majority of them were country folks, Southerners. They made fun of my accent. I pronounced my R's. First Platoon, Company C, 370th Regimental Combat Team, 92nd Infantry Division not only had a punk kid lieutenant, they had a Yankee kid lieutenant."

Receiving the Distinguished Service Cross and Divisional Cover-up

Remaining in Italy after his men and acquaintances of the 92nd Division left for the United States was an easy decision for Baker. He loathed the idea of going back home and wanted desperately to stay as long as he could in the land of the Romans. As a black man he felt more comfortable and accepted in Italy than in America. But while the idea of staying behind was appealing, he did not envision a lengthy stay either. He planned to do some sightseeing and explore the country, taking with him his German-made Leica camera.

For Second Lieutenant Baker, the end of the war in Italy also resulted in a few personal gains. By the end of May he was promoted to first lieutenant. The manner in which this event took place is somewhat interesting, but not highly unusual. As Baker recalled it, "We were sitting in a little town of Ushio, just outside Genoa. Colonel Murphy had a paper in his hand, walked in, walked over and told me: Lieutenant Baker? Now it's First Lieutenant Baker. Handed me a set of orders and a set of bars."[2]

Elated with the promotion, Baker kept his feelings to himself. Apart from being naturally reserved and quiet in disposition, he was preoccupied with other matters at the time: he wanted to remain in Italy, not go home to the United States. How that could be arranged was far more important to him than a promotion. For the next several days this was his preoccupation.

The move to Viareggio in early June would bring Lieutenant Baker an even greater surprise: the award of The Distinguished Service Cross (DSC), the nation's second highest medal for valor in combat. He remembers it this way:

> I was sitting in the company CP tent one day; an officer walked in, the Regimental S3, said: 'Hey Bake, when you going back to division? When you going to get your DSC?' First I heard of it. I was dumbfounded; didn't think I did anything that bad or good. Next day I was ordered to report to Major General Almond, the division CO. That was my first contact with him. I reported in. He said: 'I want you to write me a narrative of what happened up on that hill, and I want it day after tomorrow. I went back to company, got a typewriter and wrote what had happened. Sent the report in, and then next I heard was that on July 4 there would be a decoration ceremony.³

What transpired between early June and July 4 is a fascinating story of leadership, or the lack of it, at the level of divisional command. It is also a story that is not too difficult to piece together.

After the battle on Hill X, news of Baker's acts of gallantry began to circulate among the rank and file in the division. When General Almond heard what extraordinary feats of valor and courage Baker displayed on April 5, he was not overly enthused with the fact that one of his black junior officers had performed so heroically. General Almond, like many other senior white officers in the division, strongly embraced the idea that blacks were incapable of being good soldiers; that they lacked aggression in combat; that they were afraid of the dark and would break ranks and run in the face of enemy fire. In short, blacks could not be made into good and reliable combat soldiers. Many of these subjective and highly biased views were later incorporated in a special report that was submitted to the War Department.

At the end of June 1945 when Baker submitted his three page account of what had transpired on Hill X on April 5, General Almond, in response to a request from General Joseph McNarney, Mediterranean Theater commander, had convened a board of the division's senior white officers and asked them to prepare a report on the actions of the 92nd Infantry Division in combat. Such a report, it was felt, would be useful to the War Department which at the time was engaged in studying the post-war use of black soldiers.

Presided over by General John Wood, the board's members included regimental commanders Colonel J.D. Armstrong, Colonel James Notestein, and Colonel Raymond Sherman, Colonel William McCaffrey, the chief of staff, and Major A.D. Wilder, who had succeeded Lieutenant Colonel Edward Rowny in mid–May as commander of the 317th Engineer Combat Battalion. The board met on June 24 and 25, and put together a twenty-five page report with fifteen attached documents. Upon receipt of the report, General Almond added a long covering letter and forwarded the entire document on July 2, 1945, to General Joseph McNarney through Lieutenant General Lucian Truscott, Fifth Army commander.[4]

The report confirmed the dominant perspective or worldview shared by senior white officers in the division about black soldiers. This overarching intellectual framework lock-stitched them into a conceptual straightjacket, becoming the prism through which they viewed and evaluated black soldiers. It permeated every aspect of their analysis, leading to highly misleading and twisted conclusions. The report itself was a remarkable document, not so much for its thoroughgoing racist overtones, but for the white leadership's rejection of any responsibility on their part for the division's shortcomings. It "probably constitutes the only instance in American military history where all of the top commanders of a division placed blame for failure completely on their soldiers, rather than accepting responsibility themselves."[5] Disparaging the capabilities and combat performance of black officers, the report, at the same time, lavished praise on the behavior and fine performance of the division's white officers.

It highlighted the supposed deficiencies of black officers and enlisted men. The black officer was viewed as a "by-product of his race" in whom "servility" has been "bred … for generations." For this and other reasons, he could not become an aggressive troop leader. Moreover, the black officer's "love of exhibitionism" that stemmed

4. Vernon Baker: A Medal, a Signorina, and a New Life

from "an inherent inferiority complex" prevented him from inspiring confidence in his men. The black enlisted man, on the other hand, shows "no loyalty to fellow soldiers and abandons them on the battlefield to seek his personal safety." Further, he was "prone to distort facts or prevaricate to gain any personal advantage." Not for at least three generations, predicted the board's report, would "the essential qualities of character and stamina to produce Infantrymen ... be bred into the Negro Race."[6]

General Almond and officers of the board conceded that there were a few exceptions to this general thesis. After all it would be silly and incredulous for him and his fellow senior white officers, if they were to be taken seriously, to castigate an entire race of people with such vitriol and vituperative utterances. For example, during the division's combat operations between October 1944 and early May 1945, Almond advanced the point that "There have been many individual cases of valor or outstanding performance; however, such cases are the exceptions: the Dr. Carvers, Booker T. Washingtons, Marian Andersons of the Negro Race; they do not represent the average ability of the negro in combat."[7]

Against that background, one must approach the issue of medals of valor recommended for Lieutenant Baker and other black soldiers. Captain John Runyon, C Company commander who was with Baker during the period April 5–9, 1945, recommended Baker for the Distinguished Service Cross. In a telephone interview on September 26, 1994, Runyon confirmed that he was the one who recommended Baker for the Distinguished Service Cross.[8] When that recommendation arrived on Almond's desk, Almond requested a conference with Baker, asking the lieutenant to prepare a written report of the events of April 5. Baker submitted his account on June 12. A few days later, Almond wrote a note to the chief of staff, Colonel McCaffrey, expressing his dissatisfaction with Lieutenant Baker's account: "Send for Runyon and have him write an account of what happened to Co. C.... Baker's report says nothing except 'What I did!'"[9]

Runyon complied and wrote his report dated July 1, 1945. Both his and Baker's account constituted part of the board's report on black soldiers that was prepared and completed during the last week of June. However, Runyon's report had been edited, retyped, and backdated to

April 12, 1945. It was more than a simple act of editorial emendation. It was rather a deliberate act of clerical malfeasance by high officials, and the reasons for it are readily apparent. Captain Runyon's July 1 report was backdated because the division's commanders had already finished their report on the 92nd Division when he submitted his account of the events at Hill X. And since a very large portion of Runyon's report contradicted the prevailing view espoused by senior white officers in the division, it had to be reworked in order to match their thesis because Runyon was not going to change or alter his account.[10]

Extensive passages quoted from Runyon's July 1 report by Paul Goodman, in his study of the division titled *A Fragment of Victory*, clearly undermined the division's thesis regarding black soldiers. For that reason, these passages were purged from the April 12 version of Runyon's report. In the original account, Runyon attributed C Company's advance guard's lack of discipline (when the men failed to remain in their position near Castle Aghinolfi and bunched up under fire) not to supposedly inherent deficiencies in black soldiers, but "to the fact that many of these boys were strangers to one another and had never served together before in active combat." He offered a similar explanation for the failure of the rest of the men in C Company to move forward:

> There are few men in active combat who do not know the meaning of fear. The poorer trained the troops and the less experience they have had in fighting together, the greater degree of fear they realize.... I feel quite certain that if I could have had every man in 'C' Company with me near the castle [Aghinolfi], we could have held the ground.[11]

Runyon's implied criticism of the division's training and its reshuffling and constant shifting of personnel would seem to suggest that reasons other than racial characteristics were responsible for the poor performance of the division's black soldiers. These reasons also cast the senior white leadership in a less favorable light. Thus, those passages that contradicted the board's thesis about black soldiers were deliberately left out of the edited report. Also omitted from the board's report were some of Runyon's descriptions of Baker's heroism. His conviction that Baker would give his life to achieve the company's objective was based solely on his observations of Baker's courage and determination to fight and not on hearsay. Moreover, it was highly consistent with the lieutenant's actions before and during the phase of their withdrawal from Hill X on April 5, 1945. His heroism was such that some at the time believed that he merited the Medal of Honor.

After submitting his report in June to General Almond, Baker heard nothing more about the matter. A few days later, he was informed that there would be a decoration ceremony on July 4 and that General Truscott, Fifth Army commanding officer, would be there to pin the medals. Baker remembered the day: "General Almond received the Silver Star. I was on his left and I received the DSC.... I didn't expect that award, but what the heck."[12] Was he expecting the Medal of Honor instead? Certainly not. Baker confessed that he had absolutely no notion of any recommendation being submitted for him. He did not even know who did the recommending. When he was first interviewed in March 1994 for the Army's Medal of Honor Research Project, Vernon Baker learned for the first time that it was Captain Runyon, his white company commander, who recommended him for the Distinguished Service Cross. He was shocked.

The Distinguished Service Cross—What Is It?

Considered the second highest Army award for valor in combat in the pyramid of honors, the Distinguished Service Cross (DSC) is given for extraordinary heroism in combat against an armed enemy of the United States. It was first authorized by Act of Congress on July 9, 1918. This legislation not only clarified questions and other issues relating to the Medal of Honor, but also established for the first time in U.S. military history a secondary medal, the Distinguished Service Cross.

The creation of the DSC, it was felt at the time, would maintain and protect the exalted status of the Medal of Honor, which would be awarded only for those few truly extraordinary acts of gallantry in battle. The Committee of Military Affairs that prepared the bill stated,

"It is believed that if a secondary medal ... had been authorized in the past, the award of the ... Medal of Honor would have been more jealously guarded than it was for many years. And it is certain that the establishment of a secondary medal now will go far toward removing the temptation to laxity with regards to future awards of the greater medal."[13]

The establishment of the Distinguished Service Cross in 1918 created for the first time in American history the notion of "degrees of service to the country, each worthy of recognition, but only *one* of which could be accorded supreme recognition."[14] The Distinguished Service Cross, therefore, was juxtaposed between the Medal of Honor and the Silver Star, in order to protect the unique nature and maintain the exalted status and integrity of the Medal of Honor.

But apart from this function, the DSC was also perceived as an award of extremely high standing, and in practice, was given out in modest numbers in World War II. The report of the General Board on Awards and Decorations in the European Theater of Operations noted, for example, that "Standards for this decoration have been held extremely high, in the opinion of many, excessively so. In the European Theater of Operations, awards fell far short of the maximum number indicated in the quota system devised by 12th Army Group. It is now realized that many Silver Stars should have been Distinguished Service Crosses."[15]

By mid–1947, the United States Army had awarded 4,750 Distinguished Service Crosses to its officers and enlisted men. Of that total, black soldiers accounted for eight, or fewer than .002 percent. Early in 1946, the Negro Interest Section in the Army Bureau of Public Relations identified and published the names of five of the eight. Thirty-six years later in 1982, when the Army awarded a posthumous Distinguished Service Cross to First Lieutenant John Fox, the number of known black DSC recipients stood at six. Research for the Army Medal of Honor Archival Study in 1994 added another three names to the list, thus increasing to nine the total number of black soldiers known to have been awarded the Distinguished Service Cross in World War II.

Of the nine recipients of the Distinguished Service Cross, five were awarded posthumously. And of the four who received theirs in person, only one — Vernon Baker — did not sustain any personal injuries during the course of the action for which he was recommended for the award. While each case was judged on its own merit and differed in scope and intensity of action, all demonstrated a level of courage and gallantry that qualified them for the second highest award. The case of Private George Watson illustrates the point.

Private George Watson's display of courage is somewhat different from that of Vernon Baker. He was the first African-American soldier to earn the Distinguished Service Cross in World War II. Born in Alabama, he was inducted into the Army from Birmingham. He was initially trained at Fort Benning, Georgia, before being assigned to the 29th Quartermaster Regiment.

Watson distinguished himself by extraordinary heroism on March 8, 1943, while serving in the Pacific Command with the 2nd Battalion, 29th Quartermaster Regiment, near Porlock Harbor, New Guinea. During the morning hours on this day, he was on board a troop ship, the Dutch steamer (United States Army transport) *Jacob*, when it was attacked and severely damaged by enemy bombers. Before it sank, the ship was hastily abandoned. Many of the soldiers who jumped overboard could not swim. Private Watson was a good swimmer and instead of seeking to save his own life, he remained in deep waters frantically assisting other soldiers to reach the safety of a life raft. Weakened by continuous physical exertion and overcome by muscular fatigue, Watson drowned when the suction of the sinking ship dragged him beneath the surface of the swirling waters. This heroic action that cost him his life resulted in saving the lives of several of his comrades.

United States Army Forces Far East General Order 32, June 15, 1943, awarded Private George Watson the Distinguished Service Cross. On July 4, 1944, during a ceremony at Fort Benning, the George Watson Memorial Field, on the grounds of the Reception Center for new inductees, was dedicated to and named for the heroic black soldier, and marked with a granite rock bearing a bronze plaque. And soon after the ceremony in January 1997 in which he was awarded the Medal of Honor posthumously, a U.S. Navy transport ship was christened in his honor.

Meeting and Falling in Love with a Signorina

The war was finally over. Japan's surrender meant that American soldiers from both the European and Mediterranean theaters could now look forward to returning home. There was much jubilation as peace broke out all over Europe. But for Lieutenant Baker, the only black recipient of the Distinguished Service Cross from the 92nd Infantry Division and a little known war hero, returning to America was not one of those things he looked forward to.

He had already made up his mind; he wanted to stay in Italy for as long as he could. Toward that objective he bent his energies, exploring every available opening that the U.S. Army posted. He ended up in Viareggio, a small town along the Ligurian Sea coast and the former headquarters of the 92nd Infantry Division. Viareggio was also a seaside resort town with beautiful white sandy beaches. Here he found an opening overseeing a refinery located some miles away.

On a week of rest and recuperation ("R and R" in Army jargon), Baker and an officer friend ventured up the Ligurian coast in an American Jeep to the famed seaport city of Genoa, birthplace of Christopher Columbus. Here in this ancient city with its cobblestone streets and magnificent buildings, they planned to spend a few days relaxing in the warm Mediterranean sunshine and scouring the landscape for Italian beauties. The weather was fine. It was September and winter was still some months away. As luck would have it, no sooner had they arrived in the city than they spotted two lovely ladies strolling along the pavement to their immediate right. "What are you doing?" asked Baker in his limited Italian. "Just walking," came the curt but friendly reply. Encouraged by their reaction and wanting to seize the moment, Baker invited the two ladies for a ride in their Jeep. Quickly hopping over to the back seat, he extended a helping hand to one of them. Giovanna showed no hesitation. Her mind appeared to have been made up before the invitation was extended. She had her eyes on the young lieutenant and leapt to the back seat before her friend Marisa.

They would spend the next seven days together strolling the streets, watching the ocean waves gently lapping the sandy shore, and just staring into each other's eyes. Giovanna lived a short distance away from the Excelsior Hotel where Baker and his friend were staying. The Excelsior was reserved for black officers. Segregation, the American way, continued in Italy even after the war ended.

He would pick her up every morning and then in the evening escort her back to her home by ten. She was not allowed to visit him in his room. He looked forward to his new routine and cherished every moment of their time together. Unable to pronounce "Vernon," she settled for Fernando. They ate at the little family-operated ristorantes and pounded the cobblestoned streets of Genoa window shopping and just plain sightseeing. What they enjoyed most was being in each other's company. And for a lonely black American in a foreign land these were moments to savor. Describing her, Baker said, "She was reserved and kind, with both a strength and a softness that appealed to me in ways I can't articulate.... She filled me with this overwhelming feeling of euphoria."[16]

Baker's fun-filled week was rapidly coming to an end. He had to return to his post at camp Viareggio. But what a week it had been! Although they did not even so much as kiss each other in any passionate way, their time spent together was filled with moments of warmth and tenderness. He loved her and dreaded the moment of separation. But he also feared what her reaction would be when he contemplated telling her of his imminent departure. The moment came. It was the night before he left. Escorting Giovanna back to her house, they paused while Baker summoned the courage to break the news. "Giovanna," he stammered, "I am leaving tomorrow, in the morning." "Where are you going?" she inquired. "To Viareggio, back to the Army camp. I must return to work," replied Baker.

Expecting her to create a scene, the way lovers do when separation is at hand, he was surprised by her nonchalance. Giovanna made no fuss, taking the news in stride and demonstrating a maturity and sophistication beyond her sixteen years. She kissed him goodbye, turned around and headed straight for her door. Stunned at the sudden goodbye, Baker did not really know what to make of Giovanna's reaction. He thought for a moment whether he had done anything to upset her. Was he a failure with women? Now that he had found and fallen in love with Giovanna, he wondered if it was real. What a wonderful week he had. Would her memory vanish like her departure? His only consolation was the thought that he would have to leave Italy someday for America.

The journey back to Viareggio was uneventful. Neither man spoke much to each other. Baker was absorbed with his own thoughts, his mind playing and replaying every word and reaction that had transpired last evening between himself and Giovanna. Bewildered by her reaction to the news of his imminent departure, he nevertheless took comfort in the thought that Giovanna was different from all the other ladies he had met before. He had fallen in love with her. The pleasant memories of the week spent with her gave him some modicum of reassurance that they would meet again. Hanging on to this thought, he kept her alive in his mind. And it was not too long before hope sprang alive again.

Exactly one week after their parting, Baker was pleasantly surprised when he saw Giovanna standing at the entrance of the gate to their outpost. He could not believe his eyes. There she was, smiling and reaching out toward him. Now he knew that this was no chance encounter, she had come looking for him. He was ecstatic to see her again. Not being someone to waste time, Giovanna literally ordered him to escort her to Viareggio, a half-hour walk from the camp. The lieutenant happily complied with the order.

With his heart pounding rapidly and feet swiftly moving forward, they finally stopped in front of a three-story house. She led him into a section of the house and there it was — a two-bedroom apartment. "We live here," she announced. Baker was at a loss for words. But he quickly regained his composure when Giovanna placed her soft hands around his neck. She caressed him, their lips ventured into a journey of exploration. Describing the scene fifty years later, Baker remembered: "Her teeth playfully tugged at my ear lobe followed by the wet tip of her tongue, followed by deep, luxuriant kisses. Hands and clothing flew a dozen directions."

For the next several weeks, they lived as husband and wife in that little apartment. It was home for Baker and he enjoyed coming home to someone who was waiting for him. She was a great cook and he looked forward to her home-cooked meals. While there were some minor bumps along the road of their relationship, it was in the main pleasant and joyous.

4. Vernon Baker: A Medal, a Signorina, and a New Life

Attached to the Quartermaster Corps, a far cry from the days when he was a platoon commander on the battlefield, Baker sought ways to prolong his stay in Italy. He did not want to return to the United States. From Viareggio he went to Florence as commander of a guard detachment at a prisoner-of-war camp. Giovanna went ahead and set up house. Their stay in this magnificent city was filled with many happy and memorable days. By this time Baker had mastered the use of his German-made Leica camera. They roamed the streets of Florence, taking pictures of imposing statues and buildings, and never ceased to be amazed at the pristine beauty and splendor of this ancient merchant city made famous by the de' Medici family.

From Florence he was sent to an oil refinery at Foggia and then on to another at Bari. With each of his transfers, Giovanna went ahead and set up a home for them. In this she was very resourceful. It was now eighteen months since they had met and during this entire period, she had been his faithful companion. He appreciated her initiatives and splendid efforts at home making and deeply cherished their relationship. Reminiscing more than fifty years later Baker said, "I loved Giovanna like no other."

But their happy days were coming to an end. In December 1946 Baker received orders to leave for the United States on February 7, 1947. The news was devastating to him but not to Giovanna. In her heart she cherished the idea that they would get married and together leave Italy for America. How she loved America and wanted to go there — America of Hollywood fame where the streets are paved with gold and everyone drives a car. But try as he might, Baker could not get her to understand the complications this would impose on him, his grave concerns about "black and white" issues in America. They would not be accepted in American society — a black man with a white wife!

The more he tried to explain the realities that would confront them, the more she cried. Describing the scene, Baker said, "She cried more, kicking, screaming, flailing at me with her fists, and eventually collapsing into my arms. I cried with her, stroking her hair, struggling for reassuring words." But all he could hear her say to him was, "Fernando, you love me? Fernando, we do good in America. You take me Fernando. You take me." Baker was heartbroken. He could not bear to see her suffer this way. It was their most tender moment, recalled Baker.

Two days before his ship weighed anchor and set sail from the port of Livorno, she kissed him and said goodbye. Promising to write, she walked out of their little apartment and went home to her mother. Little did they realize then that they would never see each other again. It was a heart-rending experience for both of them. But Giovanna somehow managed to put on a brave face that painful morning. Baker spent the night companionless. It was as if Giovanna had vanished from his life. He felt the pangs of loneliness and wished that she was still around. The following day, Sunday, Baker woke up alone in their apartment. It would be his last morning in Italy. The realization of Giovanna's departure stabbed him like arrows piercing a victim's heart. Recalling that day, Baker said, "I walked around our apartment trying to impress every detail, every smell, every thought of her indelibly into my mind. Pieces of her personality were everywhere — the way the dishes were arranged in the cupboard, the neat order of things on our simple wooden table. For a moment, I saw her standing by the sink, looking at me.... Shouldering my duffel bag, I trudged to the dock with tears in my eyes. I thought my country had done it all to me before. I was wrong. I didn't know they could so effectively break two hearts."[17]

Fifty years later, Baker returned to Italy and received a hero's welcome. While there he made several attempts to locate Giovanna, but to no avail. He wanted so much to see her again, even if it would be one last time.

A Death and a New Life

Baker returned to America and started a new life. He worked for the military doing odd jobs and then with the Red Cross for several years. He also got married and raised four children. For awhile he kept up a correspondence with Giovanna, but as the years dragged on, her letters dried up and they eventually lost contact with each other. Nevertheless, he has not forgotten her and continues to cherish her memory until this day.

4. Vernon Baker: A Medal, a Signorina, and a New Life

It was February 1986 and sixty-six-year-old Vernon Baker was pleased with his life. He had been a soldier once and young, but now an old man, he was aging gracefully with only his memories to cling to. Italy was far from his mind. His children were all grown and had left home to start their own families. His wife Fern kept a busy schedule, contented and happy in her work as a swimming instructor in the community of Pacific Grove. Vernon also kept busy doing odd jobs around the house.

He had his retirement pay from the Army and his paycheck from the Red Cross. He had time to devote to his dual hobbies of hunting in the winter and skin-diving on the coast in warmer weather. His memories of that long-ago war in Italy mostly left him in a contemplative frame of mind. Vernon was a loner who preferred his own company. He seldom talked about those war memories, and then only at the prodding of one or another of his daughters who might stumble across a mention of him in some article or book about black heroes. A grandson found the case that contained the Distinguished Service Cross, asked him about it, and Baker told him: why don't you just keep that old thing.

Fern Brown, his wife of thirty-nine years, had been his faithful companion. She stood by him through thick and thin. They had raised four beautiful children, providing each with a sense of purpose and security. And together they had achieved much. Life had been good to them all these years. There was not a day when food was not on their table or the kitchen pantry empty. Now with the children all gone, they looked forward to a life of peace and quiet. Fern was sixty-eight and had been a swimming instructor for twenty-two years. They both planned on growing old together and enjoying their life in Pacific Grove. But those dreams would soon be shattered.

Out of the blue one day, Fern complained about a pain in her chest. Concerned, Baker suggested that they drive over to the base hospital where she could see the doctor. An adamant woman, stubborn as a mule when it came to visiting doctors, Fern said, "Oh no, Mister. I'm not going to any hospital. It's only a little pain." Vernon readily accepted her decision and that was the end of it. Ten days later he heard her complaining again about a pain in her chest. It was the same pain occurring at the same place. Again she brushed it off, telling him that she will be fine after a short rest. Vernon insisted this time on taking her to the doctor. She brushed him off again and requested that he take her to the PX instead.

So off to the PX they went. Baker hung around the front of the store while Fern went in by herself. When she emerged half an hour later Vernon noticed how pale his wife looked. She confessed that she was not feeling well and wanted to go home right away. "I am taking you to the hospital," Baker insisted. "No," came the emphatic reply. "I am not going to any hospital, just take me home." Again Baker complied.

On their way home about two blocks from the parking lot of the PX, Fern started to say something and then slumped forward. Gravely concerned that something serious had happened to his wife, Baker quickly swung the car around and headed toward the hospital. By the time he pulled into the emergency entrance at Fort Ord hospital, his wife was sitting up but only semiconscious. He kept blaming himself for not being more forceful with her.

The diagnosis was not conclusive, although the doctors initially suspected a heart attack. She was whisked off to a clinical room on the fourth floor for tests while Baker waited. When he was finally allowed to see her, Fern was calm, though wired to several monitors. Pleasantly surprised, Baker was pleased to see his wife looking better than when he last laid eyes on her.

Returning home alone, he was bombarded with questions from his children, who had by now made their way over to see him. Accompanied by their children LaVerne and Larise, Baker made his way over to the hospital. They stood around Fern's bedside. It was not many minutes later when a sharp pain struck again. Grabbing her chest, Fern called out for the nurse, who arrived immediately. The visitors were asked to leave the room.

They waited in silence; each had a myriad of thought crisscrossing thousands of neural pathways. What may have seemed to be an interminably long time was suddenly interrupted when a nurse appeared and called out to Vernon. Beckoning, he followed her to his wife's room. He expected the worst. Her eyes were closed and she was breathing through a respirator. The doctor confirmed that Fern had had a number of heart attacks and was now in a coma. The situation was serious. Fern never regained consciousness and within days she was dead and Vernon Baker's life was turned upside down. They had been together, a strong, loving couple, for almost forty years. "She took care of things, raised those kids, kept busy," Baker recalled fondly, adding, "She ran a tight, tight ship. She managed the money and had a good business head."

When he was interviewed at his home in Idaho, Baker, laughing, remembered how Fern came to him, after he and a good friend had gone on elk hunting excursions every winter for five straight years without bringing home even a pound of elk meat. "We got zero every year we went for five years," Baker said. "My wife said: 'The kids are all talking about how you and Mr. Byron been going hunting all these years and come back with nothing.'" She added that it seemed to her maybe there was some hanky-panky going on. Baker said if she thought that, perhaps she and Mrs. Byron should come hunting with them the next year. "So we took them hunting to Colorado and we came home with nothing," Baker recalled. "My wife said: 'I understand now. You go hunting all you want. I'm not interested in going again.'"

Alone in a big house with his grief, Baker resigned his job at the Red Cross. He was lonely and miserable. Everything seemed so pointless. Why did this have to happen to him now? Months passed with hardly any change in his mood. He felt drained of energy as if in a permanent state of lethargy. Nothing seemed to get done. This was quite unlike the Vernon Baker who was always active and never bothered by anything. The death of his wife drove him into a state of reactive depression. Luckily for him, it did not linger long enough to become chronic. He was not aware of all of this at the time, thinking instead that this mood would soon pass. And pass it did.

In the winter of 1986 Baker and a group of his regular hunting pals returned to northern Idaho, to the St. Maries area where the St. Joe and St. Maries rivers come together, for elk season. His friends talked him into going to Idaho again and he remembered how lucky they had been in that area. It did not take much to persuade him. After all, getting out of the house might do him some good, he reasoned. So off to Idaho they went. At the very least Baker thought that a change of place and scenery would take his mind off his grief, even if temporarily. Hunting still remained the one thing that appealed to him.

He loved every minute of it, particularly the moments spent waiting before taking a good shot.

They had been in camp for a week and were making an excursion into town to shop for supplies when a local resident invited them to camp on his land and hunt his property in the Benewah Valley area. They thought that this was a great idea. So at midnight they pulled camp and moved. At sunrise they awoke and beheld nature in all its glory. The Benewah Valley of Idaho is unlike California, where they lived.

It is beautiful country, thick with pine and spruce, with patches of ugliness where the timber has been clear-cut, only partly hidden by the thin fringe of trees left along the edges. Logging roads and simple dirt country roads feed into a gravel two-lane road that is eighteen miles to the blacktop in one direction, twenty miles in the other. Isolation is reality, a fact of life, especially in winter when the snow piles up eight and ten feet deep. It is a country for loners, people who are happy and feel comfortable with the distances between neighbors and don't mind a week or two here or there when they can't even get to their mailbox, much less to town.

Baker liked the look and feel of this part of the country. The steep, yet gentle foothills reminded him of parts of Italy, the type of terrain he traversed back and forth in his early manhood when he was a soldier. Moreover, the hunting ground in St. Maries (pronounced Mary's) looked like virgin territory to him. Animals seemed to be more plentiful here than in previous areas where he had hunted. And the isolation, the isolation drew him like a bee to honey. He dreamed of living in a cabin in the woods all by himself. At long last, he thought that he had found the right place where he could spend the remainder of his days. This trip was turning out to be better than he first anticipated.

Turning to their local guide, Kenny Organ, Baker asked whether he knew of any property for sale. He was interested in setting up a permanent hunting camp. Better than that, Kenny replied, "I've got the key to an unfinished cabin a quarter-mile down the road." For some time now, Kenny had been the caretaker of a house for a couple who were anxious to sell it. He gave Baker the key and told him to take a look. Baker finally walked over, several days later, and the closer he got the more interesting the place looked.

4. Vernon Baker: A Medal, a Signorina, and a New Life

The house was a modified A–frame cabin with three small bedrooms, a big living and dining area, and a good size kitchen. It was livable but nothing fancy had ever been done to it. It was unfinished but had great potential of being turned into a comfortable dwelling house. Baker and the absentee owner, now living in Spokane, negotiated by mail. Finally, he offered the man $30,000 cash for the house and five acres of land. The deal was accepted and Baker became the proud owner of a cabin located in the deep woods of Idaho, a place far removed from civilization. This was in April 1987.

The following month Baker settled his affairs in California, and gave the family house and most of his possessions to his daughters. They protested his decision and questioned his sanity. Even his hunting buddies who knew Idaho recommended against his moving. They all contended that he should go there during the hunting season but not relocate permanently. Little did the girls realize how painful it was for their father to continue living in that big house in Pacific Grove, California. It affected him greatly to have to be around a place, a house, that held so many pleasant memories of his wife Fern. "Years of losses," he said, "had taught me to find a place to leave the memories and move on."

So in May 1987, he moved to the backwoods of Idaho. He took with him some books on home improvement and carpentry. This would be his last move, the Benewah Valley his hunting ground and St. Maries his new postal address. Ten years later, it was in this neck of the woods, this home now renovated and made beautiful, where we first met Vernon Baker and his new wife. It is truly isolated, quiet, yet spectacular.

That first year he lived the solitary life and loved it. "I was by myself, free to do what I wanted to do, when I wanted to do it," Baker said. There was a deep water well and electricity, and Baker set to work renovating and prettying up the inside of the house. He added, "I didn't know what I was doing but I had my books and I was happy." So he kept busy sawing, hammering, and painting until the house began to look more and more like home. When the memories came flooding in, he would leave for long walks into the woods. There he found a safe haven, a sanctuary for reflection and healing.

He didn't make many friends that year, venturing into the old lumber mill town of St. Maries, population 2,889, only once a week. He got no strange looks, no animosity, and no curiosity. Little did the friendly faces who saw him and greeted him on the streets and in the stores realize that ten years later, this small, dignified black man would one day be elevated to the status of a national hero. All of St. Maries would be proud of him. For in their midst was a true World War II hero. People in places like St. Maries are like that, friendly but yet minding their own business. Vernon Baker reckons he was and is the only black person living in Benewah County; the U.S. Census Bureau says by its count that there are six blacks, 28 Asians, 124 Hispanics, and 602 native Americans.

Baker worked on his house and property for the next three years; he tinkered happily with an ancient surplus Army truck converted into a snowplow. He cut and split wood for the heater that kept his cabin warm when the north winds howled and the snow piled ten feet deep against the walls; he went hunting when it suited him. He said he was alone but not lonely, and far from dissatisfied with the new life he had made for himself. "I came here with the intention of spending my last days here, doing the things I had dreamed of doing as a boy," Baker said. "I work pretty hard, cutting and splitting wood but now I enjoy it. As a boy that was my chore and I hated it and swore I'd never chop another piece of wood or haul another bucket of coal." He took the time to think, read, and explore the country with an eye for good hunting areas.

In the fall of 1989 he was at the airport in Spokane, waiting to catch a plane to California to visit his new grandson, when he saw, sitting a few tables over in the lunch room, a good-looking woman. "I saw this pretty thing sitting there having lunch," Baker said. "I looked at her and she looked at me and smiled. I smiled back and started winking at her. I'd look up and she'd be looking at me and I'd wink at her." She did not return the wink. Taking his chances, he walked over and said hello and she responded with a good afternoon in a very cheerful German accent. He sat down and they talked together for over an hour, until departure time.

Concerned about the state of his eyes, she asked him if there was something wrong. "My eye? Nothing's wrong with my eye," he replied. "But you kept doing that with your eye," she asserted. Discovering that she did not know what "winking" was all about, he burst out laughing, and still does at the memory, and then explained winking to a girl named Heidi Pawlik who was traveling through, on her way back from Hawaii to her job in Bryn Mawr, Pennsylvania. She was an interior designer, a German with blonde hair and an infectious laughter. Her cheerful accent captivated him. She was a beautiful woman, sensuous, and with a wonderful personality. The minutes ticked away rapidly. Just before his flight was announced, they exchanged addresses and phone numbers and began writing and talking regularly on the telephone.

After Christmas she told Baker in a letter that the phone bills were getting too high and it was time for them to get together. He called and asked when she could take a vacation. She responded: February 10. Baker was delighted. There was deep snow on the ground and he wanted to be certain she would like the isolation of the Benewah in the dead of winter. By the time Heidi arrived, the snow on the mile-long track between Vernon's cabin and the gravel road was deep and unplowed. Baker, resplendent in a bright red snow suit, borrowed a dog sled, swaddled her in blankets, and mushed a delighted, laughing companion along the road home. "It was so romantic," she said. "He won my heart." Heidi, daughter of a German mother and a Polish father, was forty that year; Vernon Baker was 68. The difference in their ages did not matter or seem to bother them.

She stayed a week, and one day in the middle of that week she was sitting in the middle of the room under the skylight, drying her freshly washed hair in a beam of bright sunlight, while Vernon napped on the sofa. "Hasie (her pet name for Vernon), I want to tell you something," she said. "I want to come back here and stay with you." He awoke immediately. Was this for real? Boy! This is the jackpot, he told himself. He asked if she was sure. "Yes, I love this," came the reply. The week was magical with the embers of love flickering. They enjoyed being in each other's company. A week was too short; she must leave only to return.

Back in Pennsylvania she began packing and sending her clothes out to Idaho, waiting until winter ended so she could drive her car out. In May, after the thaw, Baker flew back East and helped her drive to their home. "She was a city girl, a German city girl, and completely naive about the country," Vernon said, "Everything was new and fascinating to her. I was kind of concerned at first, but she genuinely loves it." High heels slowly gave way to walking shoes and her leather jacket to woolen coats. Little by little, Heidi adjusted to her new surroundings. It was a far cry from the humdrum of city life. There was no job to go to when she got up in the morning. What a strange, but pleasant reality this was, she thought. He taught her how to cook and after a while she banned him from the kitchen.

Baker's children visited in the summer of 1993, met Heidi and invited her to California while he went hunting in the fall. "They plotted against me," he said. "When I came back marriage was in the wind. My youngest daughter, LaVerne, called and asked when I was going to marry Heidi. I said I didn't know how the kids felt about that and she said: Go for it!" It did not take much to persuade Heidi. She expected it and was very patient, waiting for the right time. It came. Vernon proposed soon after the call from his daughter and a delighted and joyful Heidi accepted.

They returned to California in November and got married in a little chapel, large enough to accommodate their families. About his marriage to a German woman, Baker loves to say: "I married the enemy." In the winter of 1993 he did. And three years later, on a cold wintry day in January 1997, Heidi was by his side at the Medal of Honor gallery in the Pentagon when Vernon Baker's plaque was unveiled.

While they were away in California exchanging marital vows, the pipes froze and they came home to find water running through the house and sheets of ice everywhere. It was a complete disaster, with water still pouring into the house from the outside well pump. The daunting task of cleaning up would take weeks. Heidi at one point suggested that they find someone to do the job. But she quickly realized that no one was around to even ask. Their honeymoon was a frozen mess. Day after day they cleaned and dried. It was work that they did not relish but they realized it had to be done. Soon the drudgery was over, making way for more pleasant things to do.

Vernon and Heidi Baker settled down to live the good life together — an interracial couple — living in an area noted for private militias and white supremacist groups. Yet they have never been made to feel like outsiders; never made to feel different or unwanted. "We have good neighbors; the salt of the earth," Baker said. As for the radicals living to the north in the Hayden Lake and Sand Point areas of the Idaho panhandle, Baker said, "As long as they don't bother me I could care less what they do. They are just fringe lunatics. Why should we worry about white supremacy when the country belongs to them anyway?"

Every fall Baker loads up his camper and battered old pickup and goes hunting. On a recent trip, while stalking an elusive elk he heard a growl, turned and saw that he was being stalked himself by a full-grown mountain lion. He wheeled and fired, and down went the prey. Mustering all his strength, he dragged the big cat out of the woods. "He's in the freezer," Baker said. "Waiting for a fellow who'll make me a rug out of his hide. If he hadn't growled he'd have had me for lunch." President Bill Clinton, during his speech at the Medal of Honor ceremony in January 1997, would make a passing reference to this incident. It elicited much laughter from the audience and brought a smile to both Vernon and Heidi.

Courage Under Fire: The Story of Lieutenant John Fox

As Christmas day 1944 approached, Allied commanders had grave concerns about an enemy attack down the Serchio Valley. It was felt that a successful German offensive would pose a serious threat to the supply base at Leghorn, crippling Allied efforts at maintaining a sustained winter operation. Rumors of an impending German assault spread through the front line companies of the 92nd Infantry Division, triggering intensive preparations. And increased road and bridge repairing activities by German engineers in their sector confirmed enemy intentions. Part of the division's plans called for a Christmas day attack on Lama di Sotto Ridge, a hilly area east of the Serchio River and a few miles from the little village of Sommocolonia where elements of the division had already taken up their positions.

Two days before the planned attack on the ridge, heavy snowfall blanketed the entire valley and exacerbated the discomfort of the troops. Persistent and lingering snow finally led to a cancellation of the attack on Christmas Eve. Meanwhile, enemy activities, including intensive preparations for an attack, continued unabated. And when anti-tank and machine gun fire were directed at their positions on Christmas night, the German response was swift and ferocious. While enemy patrols continually probed Allied positions that night, there was no close contact between them and elements of the 370th and 366th Infantry Regiments stationed in Sommocolonia, which also received its share of artillery and mortar fire. During the night, the 2nd Battalion of the 370th was hastily withdrawn, leaving only two platoons of the 366th Regiment behind to defend Sommocolonia. By early morning the 2nd Battalion had taken up defensive positions on the high ground slightly west of the Serchio River and about one mile from their original position. This tactical move would soon reveal another strategic blunder in leadership. Before daybreak the small garrison at Sommocolonia was pummeled continuously by German small arms and artillery fire for over ten minutes. From all indications, it appeared that an attack by the enemy on Sommocolonia was imminent. Had elements of the 92nd Division, i.e., the 2nd Battalion, remained in their position it was highly probable that this little village would not have fallen into enemy hands that easily.

At the time of its occupation by elements of the division, Sommocolonia, a hilltop village in the foothills of the Apennines in northern Tuscany, was a strategically commanding site with views extending all around and as far as the eyes could see. Solace Wales, an American part-time resident of Sommocolonia and author of a forthcoming book on World War II experiences of the village, provides a graphic description of this bucolic setting that has become her home for many years. "The 52 stone houses of the village, grouped together in a medieval cluster on a high promontory, look out first onto nearby flower pots and patterned vegetable gardens, and then unto the expansive Serchio Valley, and beyond to the wall of rugged peaks, the 'Apuane' mountains of marble which separate this rather remote valley from the well known Tyrrhenian Sea coast. The village was founded by the Romans who named it 'Summacolunia' meaning 'the highest colony.' At 710 meters [about 2,300 feet high], looking down on the near sea level floor, a visitor feels at the top of the world. However, Sommocolonia has not remained the highest inhabited position — there are a few nearby villages at even greater altitudes. Still, it is clear that the Romans chose their position with care as it is not only a strategic hilltop with 360 degree views and abundant spring water, but it is an especially lovely site, incorporating fields close at hand with grand vistas."[1]

It was here in this tiny hilltop village that we would first come to learn about First Lieutenant John Fox and of his heroic stance. Sommocolonia and John Fox the American hero are forever linked, and the grateful survivors of this little hamlet have not forgotten the ultimate sacrifice he made. Their munificence was artfully expressed in stone when they erected a granite monument in his honor and for the perpetuation of his memory. Any visitor to Sommocolonia today would not miss this imposing and conspicuous landmark. And for an American visitor in particular, this monument, located miles away from the beaten path, would confirm their expressions of gratitude to America. In this little act, the people of Sommocolonia have reminded us that the price of freedom is not cheap.

John Fox—The Early Years

To fully understand John Fox's decision to call for artillery fire on his position during that fateful morning in December 1944, knowing in his heart that he would die when the avalanche of shells exploded near to him, one is constrained to take a closer look at the man himself. Except for terse glimpses and a few passing remarks that appeared in newspaper articles in January 1997, very little is known or has been written about him. And the existence of that paucity was due mainly to his relegation into obscurity by the military establishment. For thirty-eight years the story recalling in detail his ultimate sacrifice on the battlefield lay buried in the 1946 publication of the U.S. Army's *Field Artillery Journal*. During this entire period also, the recommendation for the Distinguished Service Cross by a senior white battalion commander was never acted upon. So for nearly four decades, a wife and daughter lived in grief in the United States and never knew how and why their loved one died. All Mrs. Arlene Marrow Fox was left with were a pair of her husband's soiled boots, the jacket and pants he wore when he died, and the precious memories of a wonderful man she knew for less than three years.

Born May 14, 1917, into a well educated, middle-class African-American family in Lebanon, Ohio, John Fox was the first of three children. He grew up in a loving home with strict parents who instilled in him the virtues of hard work and personal integrity. When his father died while he was yet in his teens, the young Fox assumed responsibility for the well being of the family. But he also developed a passion and a strong liking for the military in his growing up years. According to his widow, "He always wanted to get into the service."[2] A bright and gifted student, young John excelled in school, particularly in math and the sciences. After graduating from high school, he sought entry into a nearby "majority" institution that had both an engineering and an ROTC program. But his application was turned down. No explanation was given. John had excellent grades and could not understand why he was not admitted into this institution. It is very clear to us today that had he been a "white kid," the situation would have been very different. But for a colored teenager growing up in America during the inter-war years, the dynamic subtleties of racial discrimination were not always readily discernible. He had worked hard and applied himself diligently and assiduously and therefore could not understand why this was happening to him. It was a devastating blow. Disappointed but not dejected, he resolved to explore other opportunities.

With a modicum of choice opened up to him, he applied to Wilberforce University, the only historically black university in his home state, and was accepted. Four years later and with his credentials in his pocket, the young Fox joined the U.S. Army in February 1941, his dream finally coming through. After graduating from Officer Candidate School at Fort Benning, Georgia, he was assigned to the 366th Infantry Regiment which, at the time, was stationed at Fort Devens, Massachusetts. Second Lieutenant John Fox slept and dreamt the military. It became his life; he was totally immersed into its culture and adapting well to military discipline. Standing slightly over six feet and well-proportioned in size, he exuded the confidence of a military officer in his bearing and manner.

Arlene Fox remembered vividly their first encounter. It was at a horse-riding venue located at Franklin Park in Dorchester. John had earlier developed an equestrian interest and was a frequent visitor of

Franklin Park. She was getting ready to saddle her horse when, out of the blue, a voice, soft and gently modulated, arrested her attention. "I'll help you with that," he said. Immersed in her thoughts and preoccupied with the task at hand, she was totally unaware that someone was standing nearby. Describing the scene fifty-seven years later, she recalled, "I turned around and there he was—tall, handsome, and smiling. He had white and perfect teeth; they were so beautiful. I got so nervous that I did not know if I could get on the horse or not."[3]

At the time of their first encounter, young Arlene was living with her parents in Brockton and working as a hairdresser in a nearby beauty salon. She knew very little about the U.S. military and never in her wildest dreams imagined herself meeting a military officer and a gentleman. Exactly two weeks later, he invited her to dinner and a movie. She accepted. John drove twenty miles to pick her up that evening for their first date. After their third date, she took him home to meet her family. Her parents were delighted to meet this young suitor who was very polished in his manners, and who they discovered was extremely respectful and courteous. John, on the other hand, was enthralled at this new development, ruminating on weightier matters of the heart.

He reasoned that Arlene must be serious about their relationship to introduce him to her parents. A few weeks later while at her home, John proposed to Arlene. She was floored. With no thoughts of marriage on her mind, she was taken by complete surprise and unable to either accept or reject his offer. There was a deafening silence; she simply did not know how to respond. But John was a very persistent man. He wanted an answer, any answer, that evening. So he drove her around Franklin Park three times during the course of that evening until she relented and said "yes." This was June 1941. Seven months later on a cold, wintry day in January 1942, they were married at the military chapel in Fort Devens. Arlene remembered: "It was a cold, beautiful day, snow was knee-deep. The ceremony was impressive and beautiful. And after we came out of the church, a bright, beautiful rainbow appeared in the clouds." It was a fitting symbol of a courtship that lasted almost nine months.

The newly married couple moved into an apartment on the post and there they set up house. Three months later Arlene became pregnant and their first and only child, Sandra Marie, was born in December 1942. The young family continued to live on base for another ten months before John left for Italy. Those were happy and fun-filled days, according to Arlene. John was a very devoted husband and a loving and caring father. He saw his daughter taking her first steps and what an impression this must have made on a young father on the eve of his departure for war in Italy. He would write to her several letters from the war zone, but the last one, dated December 15, 1944, she would always cherish. He looked forward to reuniting with his young family after the war as he had much to come home to. Clearly, this was not a man who was contemplating death. He had a young family to return to and wanted very much to be with them. "My dearest darling," he began,

> Daddy is thinking of you very much and is wishing you a very happy birthday and many, many more. Daddy is proud to have a daughter like you. Be a good girl and mind Mommy. When Daddy gets back home we will have loads of fun. Thanks, loads of cake. Tell Mommy that Daddy loves her very, very much and very deeply and wants so badly to come home to you (two). In closing Daddy wishes you and Mommy many happy returns of the day.
> Loads of love and kisses to you both.
> Love,
> Daddy.[4]

The Attack on Sommocolonia

Several days before German troops, dressed as partisans, infiltrated this hilltop village, First Lieutenant John Fox of Cannon Company, 366th Infantry Regiment, was getting himself ready for a critical mission that was fraught with danger. He was assigned the task of forward observer for the 598th Field Artillery Battalion in Sommocolonia. The preparation for this assignment called for a familiarization with outpost support services and the techniques involved in maximizing the effective use of close-in artillery support fire. The use of artillery fire in its support role of ground troops was a cornerstone of American tactics during World War II. But the use of artillery fire, to be efficacious and devastating to the enemy, must be precise and well controlled. Artillery equipment required adjustments every morning and throughout the day depending on target changes and weather conditions. And artillery fire must also be controlled within one hundred yards of forward troops in order to avoid casualties by friendly fire. Fox had to learn these techniques and to familiarize himself generally with artillery fire controls for the mission he was about to undertake. Shoddy work on his part, the miscalculation of distances, could mean life or death for many of his own comrades. On the other hand, accurate timing and precise measurements could wreak havoc on the enemy.

He and his aide, a noncommissioned officer, spent two days with elements of the division's 598th Field Artillery Battalion stationed at Barga, exactly two miles southwest of Sommocolonia. Sergeant William Wyatt, team leader in charge of the day's operation when Fox and his aide turned up, recalled the events very vividly: "During the two or more days Lieutenant Fox was with me we rehearsed every detail he could think of or that I could think of to bring to his attention. In that short time we became friends. I found Lieutenant Fox to be extremely intelligent, one of the most gentle persons you could hope to meet, a model gentleman if there is such a person. He showed me pictures of his young family, his beautiful wife and young child. They obviously were close to his heart. When Lieutenant Fox headed out for Sommocolonia, I could not help but experience a sense of sadness because here he was heading for a rugged peak and I was sure he was carrying in his heart a sense of loneliness for his lovely young family. This is what makes the incident of that morning so unforgettable."[5]

Arriving in Sommocolonia a day before the village came under enemy attack, Lieutenant Fox and his aide took up a strategic position in a tower, lateral to a position occupied by elements of the 598th Field Artillery Battalion at Barga. During the night, hundreds of enemy soldiers, dressed as partisans, began to pour into the village. The Italian partisans during World War II were former soldiers who were cut off from their homes but still in possession of their weapons. Many of them, young and patriotic, fled from Mussolini's attempts to conscript them; others were urban evacuees or released prisoners of war. They were most active during the summertime, finding support among village peasants. Vigorously opposed to German occupation of Italy, they constantly harassed and tied down German troops for days. They fought as guerrillas and on the side of the Allies. Cognizant of their role and mission, the Germans thought it wise to conceal the true identity of the men they were dispatching to seize Sommocolonia. The attempt was successful.

Daybreak found hundreds of enemy soldiers in and around the village. Between 5 and 7 a.m., Austrian troops and Italian Fascists, elements of the German army, now dressed in their respective uniforms, appeared like demons out of the blue and savagely attacked this tiny hamlet. At the commencement of this attack, the 92nd Reconnaissance Troop, stationed nearby to the east at Bebbio, was ordered by the 370th Regiment to withdraw to Coreglia, a prepared position south of Sommocolonia (see map insert). Overwhelmed by enemy soldiers, the situation in the village rapidly deteriorated. By 7:35 a.m., Lieutenant Graham Jenkins of G Company 366th Regiment called for reinforcements. The 2nd Battalion commander immediately ordered a platoon of E Company to Sommocolonia.[6] Jenkins later reported street fighting from door to door and requested mortar and artillery support fire. Reinforcement, arriving a little too late and in such a small number, was simply unable to turn the tide of battle on the ground. The situation grew progressively worse despite courageous efforts by dozens of the real Italian partisans who by now had engaged the enemy in hand to hand combat.

Meanwhile, elements of the 366th Infantry Regiment, outnumbered and in a state of slight confusion as to the true identity of partisans, fought desperately to repel the invaders. But it was too late. From his commanding position, Lieutenant Fox had a good sense of the situation on the ground. He saw the fighting and fully recognized the hopeless condition they were in. He also knew that he and his aide had ample time to withdraw unscathed before the enemy came beating down his door. It was only a matter of minutes. For him, withdrawal was not an option. He continued to call for artillery fire. As the fighting intensified, with enemy soldiers swirling around his building, some having already cleared the first floor, Fox maintained a level head

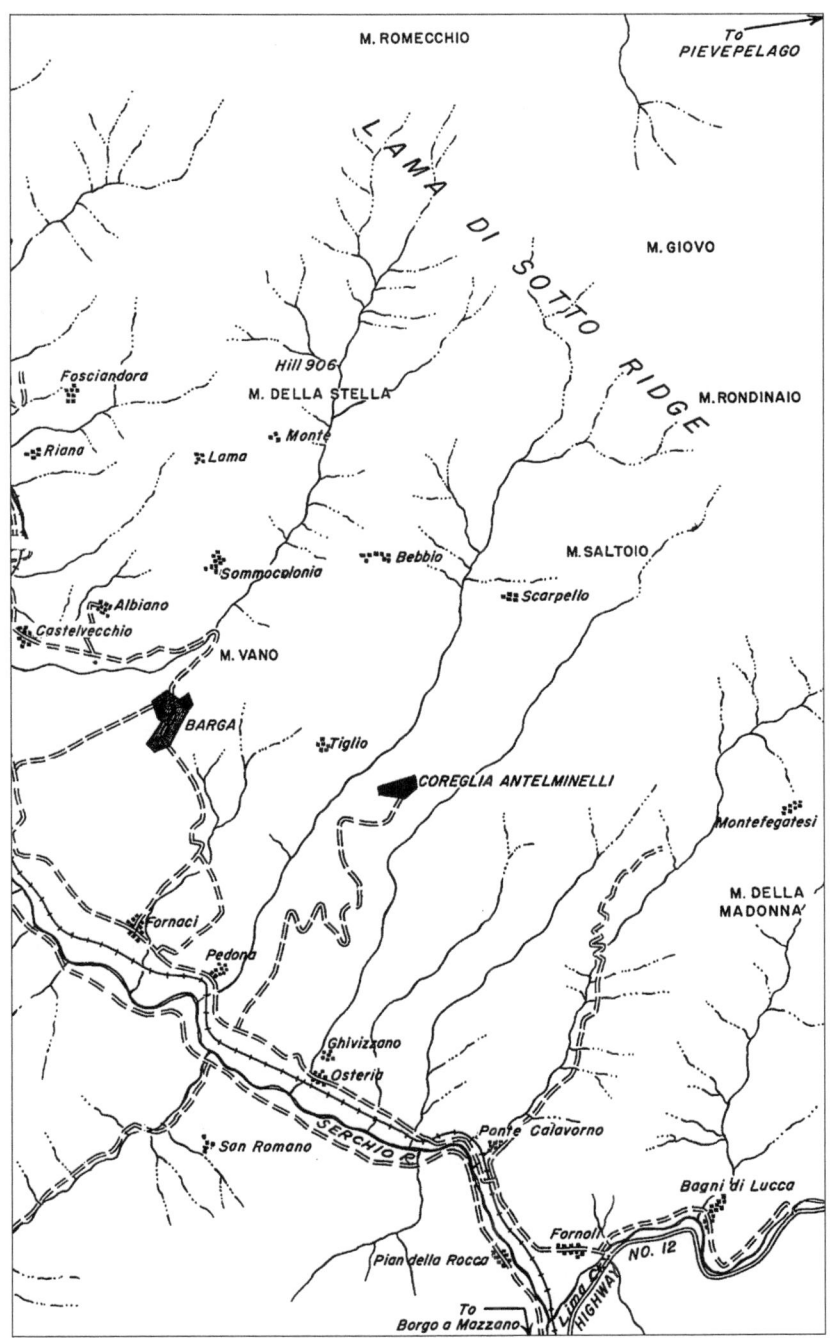

The Serchio Valley Sector

and was not about to give up. Sensing the imminence of death, he determined to strike a deadly blow to the enemy.

As the enemy, about a hundred in strength, closed in on him, Fox quickly radioed the 598th's Fire Detection Center (FDC) again, and this time made a highly unusual request: "That [last] round is just where I want it — bring it in sixty more yards." A forward adjustment of sixty yards would land shells on the building he and his aide were occupying. He reasoned that the only way to stop the enemy was to call for artillery fire on his position. He made another call, requesting for a smoke screen to cover the withdrawal of the remaining men of the 366th Infantry who by now were beating a hasty retreat. The FDC duty officer who received the "unusual" message was stunned.

Aware of the gravity of the situation and sensing the urgency in Fox's voice, he immediately called the Field Artillery Battalion commander and informed him of the lieutenant's request. The commander, in turn, radioed Fox to verify for himself that the request was authentic and that the coordinates were correct. Fox's request was to have the next barrage of artillery shells dropped directly on the building he was occupying. Time was a critical factor in this operation as further delay would result in death for him and his aide at the hands of the enemy. To the commander he snapped: "Fire it! There are more of them than there are of us. Put fire on my OP [Observation Post]."[7] Without further hesitation the 598th fired a volley consisting of twelve rounds of 105mm high explosives on the target. The tower-like building, used as an observation post, was immediately demolished, instantly killing Lt. John Fox and his aide as well as scores of enemy soldiers. In this heroic act of self-sacrifice, John Fox accounted for more enemy deaths than when he was alive.

Emboldened by their initial success at Sommocolonia and its environs, the Germans continued their offensive with unrelenting fury for several more days. This necessitated a number of changes in redeployment of forces by the 92nd Division and the introduction of the 8th Indian Division into the fray. In the early afternoon on December 27, the Indian Division took control and command of the entire Serchio sector, replacing the 370th Regiment. Retaining the 598th Field Artillery Battalion, which had stood firm against German resistance, they immediately went into action. On the 29th the 370th Infantry went into operational control of the 8th Indian Division. Meanwhile, as Allied fighter bombers continued to attack and destroy enemy positions in the Serchio Valley, the Germans began to retreat. Indian troops cleared the town of Barga on the 29th and Sommocolonia on the 30th. By New Year's day 1945, the 92nd Division's lines were practically restored, the German attack finally dissipated.

The 92nd Division's failure to repel this German attack in the Serchio Valley lay squarely at the feet of leadership ineptitude. It was not a surprise attack that dropped as bolts from the sky. Rather, its preparation was common knowledge and its imminent commencement correctly anticipated. Fully cognizant of these developments, General Almond blundered again in his deployment and strategy. In a postwar interrogation of Brigadier General Fretter Pico, commanding general of the German 148th Infantry Division that attacked the 92nd in the Serchio Valley, explained how they perceived the situation and how they exploited its weakness. He remarked quite succinctly that "The weaknesses of your [meaning Almond's] deployment in the Serchio Valley in December 1944 were that your troops were deployed on a front which was too long for the number of troops available, and your reserves were too far in the rear areas which prevented their being deployed immediately."[8] That Almond failed again, this time to commit sufficient troops to meet and repel a fierce German attack that was building up for days, an attack that he knew would be unleashed with fury, was inexcusable. His strategic leadership blunder resulted in scores of dead American soldiers, and not the least, in the perpetuation of the view that blacks cannot stand up and fight aggressively in combat.

Leadership Inertia

For his extraordinary courage and gallantry in the face of enemy fire, the artillery commander, Brigadier General William Colbern, recommended Lieutenant John Fox for the Distinguished Service Cross.[9] Moreover, several witnesses testified that they saw the recommendation. The action mentioning the recommendation of a DSC for

Lieutenant Fox was described in detail in the January 1946 issue of the Army's *Field Artillery Journal*. It stated in part:

> One of the forward observers showed unbeatable heroism. Lieutenant Fox and his party had ample time to pull out. They remained on the second floor of a house directing defensive fires until only a handful of defenders remained. As the enemy closed in, Lieutenant Fox called for artillery fire increasingly close to his own position. One of his last requests for fire included a target only 60 yards from him. The enemy continued to press forward in large numbers. When the house ... was entirely surrounded, he called for fire directly on it. He was questioned as to whether the mission was safe to fire it. He answered, "Fire it! There's more of them than there are of us." He was recommended posthumously for the Distinguished Service Cross.[10]

But either lost or destroyed, the recommendation was never acted upon. The issue for serious consideration is neither the veracity of Fox's heroism nor the existence of the recommendation of a Distinguished Service Cross for him. What has not been fully explained is why the recommendation for Fox was not forwarded by General Almond to Fifth Army. This was the usual procedure and in most cases was strictly adhered to. Explanations abound. Some have suggested that it was inadvertently lost or simply not acted upon. Others have offered the view that the omission was deliberate — either because Fox was black or, in one arcane twist, because commanders wanted to cover up the mistaken bombing of black American troops in the village by Allied aircraft. Whatever happened to Lieutenant Fox's recommendation will never be known. However, another explanation, quite consistent with General Almond's views and assessment about top awards, and the nascent thesis about black soldiers, may answer this recalcitrant question.

Throughout the Italian Campaign General Almond adopted an inexorable attitude toward black soldiers and in particular toward recommendations for higher military awards. This unyielding disposition, continual in its manifestation and deleterious to troop morale, played an important role in his evaluation of awards. Almond held the view that a failed mission ought not to result in awards for valor in combat regardless of the display of feats of courage or dazzling performance by individual soldiers. On more than one occasion he demonstrated this tendency.

The case of Captain Walter Dabney of B Company, 366th Infantry Regiment, is instructive. For his gallantry in action on December 5, 1944, Captain Dabney was recommended for the Silver Star. Almond refused to approve it. He subsequently ordered an investigation into the events of Dabney's actions, this time utilizing the services of the division's inspector general.[11] The officer who conducted the investigation did a thorough job and recommended that Captain Dabney be awarded the Silver Star. In his letter of recommendation he said, "Captain Dabney [should] be commended for his actions which were a source of inspiration to those around him."[12] In spite of this impartial investigation which he initiated, General Almond did not budge, stubbornly refusing to change his mind and approve the recommendation. Explaining this recalcitrant posture, Colonel William McCaffrey, the division's chief of staff, stated quite succinctly that the "results of the mission were unsatisfactory to the division commander."[13]

For General Almond, what mattered most was the conduct and success of the overall mission and not so much the individual acts of heroism. In short, if individual acts of valor occurred within the context of a failed mission, he was loath to approve recommendations for higher awards. In Lieutenant Fox's case, he behaved differently; he exceeded his authority. It was within his ambit to disapprove a higher awards recommendation, but having done so, he was obligated to pass it on to the higher echelon in the chain of command, which in this case was the U.S. Fifth Army. Thus the issue of his disapproval was immaterial. What was clearly relevant in this case was his obligation to forward the recommendation, a duty he failed to discharge with probity, and instead, relied on his procrustean tendency.

While Almond recognized that Fox's display of courage and gallantry in combat were remarkable, it nevertheless took place, in his estimation, within the context of a disastrous mission failure. According to one report that Almond adhered to, black soldiers of the 366th Infantry Regiment stationed in Sommocolonia on the morning of December 26 refused to engage the enemy in any fire fights. They decided instead to take refuge in abandoned homes. Moreover, the disorderly withdrawal of the regiment's 2nd Battalion also annealed his resolve.[14] Thus he declined to endorse Colbern's recommendation of the DSC for Lieutenant Fox or to even forward it to Fifth Army with his disapproval.

Buried Treasure and Hope

For thirty-eight years the story of Lieutenant John Fox's heroism in the tiny village of Sommocolonia lay buried under a pile of bureaucratic corrosiveness. While this ostensible lack of concern was neither intentional nor deliberate on the part of the Army Awards Branch, it nevertheless underscored the enormity and delicate nature of the tasks they deal with on a daily basis. Simply put, the John Fox case did not surface as an issue to be investigated and resolved because no one brought it to their attention in any meaningful and compelling way. Several senior white officers, including Colonel McCaffrey and General Almond, who survived the war and returned to America, initiated no inquiries into the matter. According to McCaffrey, they simply wanted to get on with their lives and not be bothered with bygones in Italy.[15] But there was one group, veterans of the 92nd Infantry Division, who in their annual reunions, never failed to mention or recall the display of courage by Lieutenant John Fox in Sommocolonia. They kept his story and his memory alive. And year after year these men and their wives would meet and share stories about the war in Italy.

One of their comrades, a veteran of the 92nd who also fought in Italy, would assist in bringing closure to the Fox's case. Hondon Hargrove, a modest man and a historian, was determined to right this particular wrong. Returning to America after the war, he learned even more about the display of courage and the manner in which Lieutenant Fox died. He also heard about a recommendation of a Distinguished Service Cross for Fox. But with no hard evidence in hand, he was constrained in his range of action given his preoccupation at the time with raising a family and the pursuit of higher education.

In the late 1970s, Hargrove contemplated writing a book on the

5. Courage Under Fire: The Story of Lieutenant John Fox

92nd Infantry Division in Italy. This venture would take him to the National Archives located at the time in Suitland, Maryland, and to several other repositories where valuable information was unearthed. Not long after he embarked on this research effort, Hargrove stumbled across a treasure trove regarding the Fox case. From eyewitnesses' accounts and from historical documentation, he carefully and painstakingly built a compelling case. In his mind there was no obfuscating issue that could now stand in the way. Armed with a complete dossier on Lieutenant John Fox, Hargrove presented his findings to Major Robert Roush at the Army Awards Branch in Alexandria, Virginia. While sympathetic to the case, Roush had to operate within policy guidelines and other constraints. The fact that a recommendation was submitted by the commander of the 598th Artillery Battalion for the Distinguished Service Cross in this instance made Fox's case much easier to prosecute. Hargrove, meanwhile, continued his correspondence with the Army Awards Branch, and in a letter to Major Roush dated September 15, 1980, he reiterated Fifth Army's policy regarding command channel procedures of award recommendations.

The Awards Branch conducted its own research into the case and afterward made a positive recommendation of a Distinguished Service Cross for Lieutenant John Fox to the Secretary of the Army. When the final hurdle was cleared, one involving Congressional approval on the statute of limitation, Lieutenant Fox was awarded the Distinguished Service Cross posthumously on April 1, 1982, exactly thirty-nine years after he died a heroic, self-sacrificing death. The award was presented to his wife, Mrs. Arlene Fox, in a ceremony at Fort Devens, Massachusetts, where Fox had joined the 366th Infantry Regiment. In attendance also were surviving members of the 366th and the 92nd Infantry Division. Relieved and somewhat pleased, these aging veterans believed that complete justice was still not done. The outcome that would bring closure to this case would be the award of the Medal of Honor to their fallen comrade. Grateful at the result of round one, they patiently awaited round two which, when it finally came in January 1997, completely vindicated their long, arduous struggle.

Explaining Fox's Self-Sacrificing Action

Many people take risks in life. It is a necessary part of living. But most, if not all, of those risks we take do not include the certainty of death in our calculation. By nature we are a self-preservation species. In short, most of us take only calculated risks in life. When John Fox called artillery fire on his position over half a century ago, he was not taking a risk. He did not believe for a moment that he would escape death, so go ahead and take a chance. He knew that death would be certain. The question that many have asked was why he did it knowing that he would die? This was a man who just a few days before had written a beautiful and moving letter to his daughter and wife, telling them how much he loved them and reassuring them that he would be coming home soon.

I have struggled for an answer since I first came across the story and circumstances surrounding John Fox's death but could not find a plausible one until I met Mrs. Arlene Fox during the Medal of Honor ceremony at the White House on January 17, 1997. A small, graceful, and charming woman, Arlene Fox was easy to talk to. A retired nurse from the VA Hospital in Brockton, Massachusetts, with twenty-nine years of service under her belt, Mrs. Fox had a real and difficult struggle in life after her young husband died on Christmas Day 1944. Facing severe financial constraints at the time, she nevertheless determined to quit her job as a hairdresser and pursue a nursing career. Working hard and applying herself diligently to her studies, she completed her program and secured a job at the VA Hospital. Although she had ample evidence that her husband was killed in action in Italy, she clung to the belief that perhaps the Army somehow had made a mistake and that John was still alive and would turn up one day at this hospital. She wanted to be there when he came. And it was this very hope that her husband would one day return that kept her year after year at this hospital.

After Lieutenant Fox departed for Italy, Arlene and their infant daughter Sandra continued to live on the base at Fort Devens. She remembered vividly the events of that week when she first received notice that her husband was missing in action. Two nights before she received that first letter, she had a dream and all she could see in that dream were his hands. In the morning and throughout the day she had an uncanny feeling that something terribly bad had happened to her husband. She felt that the worse had occurred. The following day, cold and snowing, Arlene saw a mail carrier from the telegraph office coming up her driveway. The woman was crying. In her hand she had a letter for Mrs. Fox. It stated that "Lieutenant John Fox was missing in action." There was bad news all around the post, many wives were crying and in a state of depression, according to Arlene. Two weeks later, she received another letter confirming that her husband had died in combat. There was no explanation, no details, just this simple statement from the Army.

When the opportunity to engage her in a conversation presented itself on that very busy and hectic day at the White House, I straightaway asked her the inevitable question. Without a moment's hesitation she answered, "Knowing John, it was reduced to one option, let it count for something."[16] "Wow," I said, immediately understanding why he did it. Her answer made sense. If he were going down, if death was certain and staring him in the face, then he would go down in a blaze carrying with him scores of enemy soldiers. In short, his death, real and imminent, must count for something worthwhile. This was indeed a self-sacrificing death for one's country. Several veterans of the 92nd Division, including a few who knew Lieutenant John Fox well, confirmed that he was an extraordinary officer, a soldier completely devoted to the military. But none of them ever imagined that he would step out of the "box" and sacrifice his life. One of Fox's good friends, a fellow officer named Otis Zackary who lives in Los Angeles, recalls with great pain the memorable events of that fateful day. John's death in Sommocolonia, according to him, was the ultimate sacrifice a soldier could make for his country. But he also did not conceive of it the way Mrs. Fox did. Her explanation, a model of sagacious brevity, chimed well the Biblical story of Samson at the moment of his death in the Philistine temple. Unable to extricate himself from the enemy's hold, Samson, facing inevitable death, prayed and asked God for superhuman strength just one more time. When those lofty columns and impregnable walls of the Philistine's temple came tumbling down like a veritable Niagara of cascading rocks, Samson's certain death accounted for the demise of thousands of Israel's enemies.

Fifty-two years later a grateful nation remembered Lieutenant John Fox and bestowed upon him posthumously its highest award for gallantry in combat, the Medal of Honor. His friend Otis Zackary was also there to witness and share with his wife Arlene, daughter Sandra, and granddaughter Cassandra, this final and blissful moment.

6

THE LONG ROAD TO RECOGNITION

By the end of World War II, the United States Army had awarded 294 Medals of Honor to officers and enlisted men who had fought in the three theaters of operations and the Pacific Command. Of that number, not one was awarded to a black soldier although more than 50,000 blacks had been engaged in actual combat against the enemy. Concerns were soon raised about the conspicuous absence of even one black recipient of the Medal of Honor. As early as 1946, Dr. C.F. Hopson of West Virginia wrote a letter to President Harry Truman in which he pointed out the absence of a black Medal of Honor recipient and called for an immediate inquiry.[1] These concerns never faded; they were kept alive throughout the years in sections of the media, in individual letter-writing efforts to politicians and senior Army brass, and in annual reunions of black veterans across the country, particularly the 92nd Infantry Division.

Veterans of the 92nd Infantry Division, under the dynamic leadership of stalwarts such as Jehu Hunter and the unit's unofficial historian, Col. Major Clark, never relented in their struggle to keep this issue alive. To them and all black veterans of World War II, the apparent continuous denial of the nation's highest award for gallantry in combat to at least one of their fellow black comrades meant that black participation in World War II was mere tokenism and not meaningful; that their spent lives were all in vain, and that their efforts counted for naught. It also signaled to them an inexplicable recalcitrance on the part of whites to correct an act of injustice. This complete lack of enthusiasm on the part of the Army Awards Branch to correct this problem they could not understand. For them, the award of a Medal of Honor to a World War II black soldier would mean a total vindication of their cherished belief that blacks not only fought with great courage and heart to defend the lofty principles upon which this country was founded, but demonstrated individual acts of extraordinary bravery that merited the nation's highest honor.

During World War II and after, knowledgeable people in the services and outside, and in numerous black communities across this nation, charged that racism in the Army, either as a matter of policy or by the actions of individual white officers in the chain of command — or both — had prevented black soldiers from being recognized for valor in combat by the award of the Medal of Honor. Charges of white racism were indeed compelling and not simply an escalation of rhetoric and a heightened emotional state. Many of the concerns raised were also based on the more substantive issue of "black" combat performance before, during, and after this particular war. Historians today agree that blacks who served from the earliest times in American history in various branches of the Armed Forces did so with pride and distinction. And while many served in the colonial wars, the war for independence, and subsequent conflicts, it was not until the Civil War that large numbers experienced combat in all its dimensions in units segregated by race.

Between the end of the Civil War and the 19th century, thousands of blacks served honorably and effectively during the Indian wars and in the conflict with Spain and in the Philippines. In World War I, blacks again served in combat in both the 92nd and 93rd Infantry Divisions and in units attached to allied armies in France and elsewhere. World War II was no exception. When the ice was finally broken to allow blacks into combat, thousands of them served individually and in segregated units up to division strength in the Army Ground Forces, Army Air Forces, and the Navy. Overwhelmingly though, their service was within a rigid framework of segregation. And in spite of this crippling constraint, many black soldiers fought with courage, tenacity, and skill.

Setting the Record Straight

The end of World War II marked the beginning of a long and arduous struggle for fair and proper recognition of black soldiers who fought bravely alongside white American troops. Decades would pass before any real attempt was made to breathe new life into a comatose idea.

In 1990, John Shannon, then acting secretary of the Army, ordered that an archival research be undertaken to determine whether any black soldier in World War II had actually been recommended for the Medal of Honor and, if one or more recommendations could be found, then search for the reason(s) why those recommendations had not been processed. The research would also determine whether the failure to process a "recommendation" constituted a violation of War Department regulations or public law. In short, the study was very narrowly defined with an emphasis placed on combing the records to find an unprocessed recommendation of the Medal of Honor for a black soldier.

With a Statement of Work in hand delineating a clearly defined task and an amount of money set aside, a Request for Proposal (RFP) was finally drafted by the Army Contract Section in the Pentagon. Secretary Shannon made it abundantly clear to his subordinates that he wanted this effort to be a "set-aside." That is, only historically black colleges and universities would be eligible to respond with a proposal. However, before the request was disseminated to black colleges and universities, Sadaam Hussein invaded Kuwait. Preoccupied with far more weighty and strategic matters, the Army placed the Medal of Honor project temporarily on the back burner.

In early 1993, with the Gulf War over and the country again at peace, the project was dusted off and RFPs sent to all 104 black colleges and universities. At the time, the author was an assistant professor of international relations at Shaw University in Raleigh, North Carolina, making preparations to attend an intensive five-week training program in military history at West Point. Passing the office of the vice president for academic affairs one day in April, he was invited in and given a huge document to look over. The vice president said, "I want you to take a look at this and give me a response." The author examined the document in detail and made a few phone calls.

One of those calls was to Dr. Richard Kohn, a former chief of U.S. Air Force History at the Pentagon between 1982 and 1992 and currently a professor of military history at the University of North Carolina, Chapel Hill. When they met in the senior commons room at Chapel Hill, Dr. Kohn persuaded him to drop the idea of responding with a proposal saying, in effect, that the Army was definitely not interested in making amends to black soldiers after all these years. Besides, he indicated, this is a political stunt; nothing would come out of it. The author had lunch with Dr. Kohn and pressed the issue. Kohn finally relented and told him to contact Colonel John Cash in Washington, D.C. He complied.

After contacting Colonel Cash, the author secured the help of the academic vice president, Dr. McLouis Clayton, and persuaded the president of Shaw University to fork out some money in order to invite Colonel Cash and others to a preliminary meeting at Shaw. The meeting was helpful in clearing up some questions about the Army's request for a proposal, and in securing the agreement of both Kohn and Cash to join the research team. He then wrote and rewrote the proposal while at West Point. Kohn edited the final draft, making it more technically sophisticated, yet readable and in conformity with the Statement of Work. The end product turned out to be a concise, strong proposal.

Added to the Shaw University team of researchers during this period were Colonel Elliott Converse, Ph.D., and Colonel Robert Griffith, Ph.D. After passing through two rounds of technical questions and the submission of a best and final offer, Shaw University was awarded a contract for $320,585 on September 27, 1993. Quotations from other competitors ranged from $695,000 to $1.2 million, the latter reflecting a joint effort by Morgan State and Howard universities. The author assumed the roles of principal investigator and project manager. The work of the Shaw team would occupy the better part of two years. Extended periods were spent scouring the National Archives and the United States Army Institute of Military History. Over forty individuals were interviewed and many speeches given during this period. In the end, the team produced a thoroughly researched and very comprehensive report.

A highlight of the effort came in April 1994 when the author and Colonel Cash met and interviewed Vernon Baker in Spokane, Washington, for the first time. The interview was very eventful. Baker's wife, Heidi, accompanied him to the interview. Standing five feet seven inches tall and weighing not more than 150 pounds, Baker bore himself with grace and dignity and exuded a quiet confidence. He spoke slowly, carefully choosing his words. When he was asked to describe the battle at Hill X on the morning of April 5, 1945, both Cash and the author were surprised by the excellence and clarity of Baker's memory.

His description of those long-ago events matched almost perfectly, word for word, the three-page account Baker had written for General Almond during the last week of June 1945. Baker did not have a copy of that report in his possession; the author gave him one afterward. Later during the day Colonel Cash remarked to the author, "You must recommend him for the medal. He is a sure candidate." At the end of an hour and a half interview, the author turned to Baker and asked, "Mr. Baker, what was it that made you fight so courageously given the treatment of blacks in America?" Unable to maintain his placid composure any longer, Baker burst into tears; his voice choked with emotions when he said simply: "I did it for my men." Seeing the state of her husband, Heidi Baker also burst into tears. The interview temporarily halted, there was not a dry eye in that room. The four of them met again the following day. On this occasion it was more pleasant and far less heart wrenching.

Seven months into the research, the Shaw University team was satisfied that no unprocessed paperwork recommending a black soldier for the Medal of Honor during World War II existed in the military archives at Suitland, Maryland or anywhere else. They were disappointed, but by now hardly surprised. They believed that the Army during World War II had a deliberate policy to exclude blacks from receiving the Medal of Honor, hence the absence of a recommendation. When the author reported his latest findings and current state of the research to the colonel in charge of the project at the Army Awards Branch in Virginia, she told him to write the final report and bring the research to a close. Dr. Kohn accompanied the author on this visit. After they left the colonel's office and were in the parking lot at the nearby Holiday Inn, Kohn turned to him and said, "Dan, you are too naïve. The Army was not interested in this from day one." Disappointed, the author began to look for some way to keep the study alive and at the same time make a compelling case to the Army for acting to redress an old wrong.

He recalled that one of his researchers had sent him a copy of a letter that he found in the archives. In the letter written by General Eisenhower, instructions were given to reexamine the best Distinguished Service Cross cases in the Mediterranean Theater of Operations with a view to upgrading some to the Medal of Honor. At the end of this exercise, four DSC cases were approved by the War Department and upgraded to the Medal of Honor. While this information was useful, it did not seem sufficient to make a compelling case for a reexamination of black DSC recipients. He needed another precedent.

Soon after, the author made a research trip to the George Marshall Library in Virginia. During his second day of research, he found an old Army publication on the history and development of the Medal of Honor. Armed with a small photocopier, he copied the entire document and devoured the contents during most of that night at his hotel. To his amazement and delight, he found exactly what he was looking for. Another instance of reexamination of DSC cases took place after Armistice in World War I. General Blackjack Pershing questioned the parsimony of Medals of Honor before Armistice and ordered that a thorough reexamination of DSC cases be undertaken with a view to upgrading the most compelling ones to the Medal of Honor. This exercise resulted in 78 cases being upgraded to the Medal of Honor, bringing the total to 95 for World War I.

Armed with these two precedents, the author once again approached the colonel and made his argument for a similar reexamination of the nine black DSC cases of World War II. The colonel agreed and the research effort proceeded on a different course. The first draft of the final product was submitted in August. Both the author and Kohn discussed it and knew that it would not pass muster because two of the seven chapters revealed inadequate research work. The team requested an extension to December 1994. The task at hand required that more archival work needed to be done on these two chapters. It was quickly undertaken and the exercise proved tremendously beneficial to the overall project.

Chapter 5, one of the two chapters that had to be rewritten, turned out in the end to eloquently underscore the depth of racism senior white officers demonstrated in their handling of black troops during World War II. The entire study was completed on schedule. Dr. Elliott Converse, one of the researchers, painstakingly built and supported the thesis that it was the deeply held racist views of senior white commanders of the 92nd Infantry Division that influenced the awards process rather than the combat performance of individual black officers and enlisted men. The leadership of the division saw itself as reporting the results of an experiment. Thus the constant objective and preoccupation of top commanders was to collect, evaluate, and draw conclusions from firsthand and at-the-time data which could be relied upon by the War Department in its employment of Negro military manpower in the future. Chapter 5 exposed the rigidities of Army segregation, its stifling effects, and devastating impacts on black morale and performance. It made an even stronger case.

On January 18, 1995, the author drove to the Army Awards Branch in Arlington, Virginia, and handed six copies of the study along with tapes and other case materials to the contracting officer. It was a sunny day. The roads were free of snow. Coming over to see him that day from the Pentagon's contract office was Harry Shatto, administrative contracting officer for this project. From the early days of the investigation, Shatto had shown a keen interest in the research. Today he made this special trip just to receive his personal copy of the report. The report made a compelling case for the Army to investigate upgrading black DSC awards from World War II to Medals of Honor. It also made a strong case for a Medal of Honor for Staff Sergeant Ruben Rivers, a Silver Star recipient.

The Long Wait

After submission of the study, a long waiting period followed before the Army took action. Secretary of the Army Togo D. West announced that the Army would now convene a Decorations Board to evaluate the recommendations contained in the Shaw Study. The Army Awards Branch did a thorough job assessing the study. They checked every fact, made detailed notations of every case, and examined the narrative for accuracy and consistency. At one point, the Army lawyers wanted to know whether Staff Sergeant Edward Carter, one of the ten cases recommended for the medal by the study, continued to face the enemy when he crossed an open field making his way back to his company headquarters, taking two prisoners with him. They were assured that he did. Edward Carter's case is a most interesting one.

A special investigative report by Joe Galloway, undertaken two years after the award of Carter's Medal of Honor, ran as a cover story in the May 31, 1999, issue of *U.S. News & World Report*. The story that unfolded in Galloway's report quintessentially underscored the finest soldiering qualities of Eddie Carter, his gallantry and ability to fight, and also his love for his country. But the report also exposed the strictures of a corrosive bureaucracy caught in the grip of a communist paranoia, and how misinformation could destroy someone's life. Carter, a war hero and American patriot, was in the end destroyed by a state machinery that spun out of control. It was reminiscent of the McCarthy era when anyone who was even remotely suspected of espousing communist sentiments in this country was in constant fear of having his or her life destroyed. That a country which prided itself in its respect for law and order and in its constitutional guarantees of individual freedoms and liberty could behave in such a draconian way was indeed mystifying to civilized man.

The year ended with no firm decision of the outcome. The Army, it was believed, was taking its time on this one. It would not bow to any form of political pressure. Attempts by concerned congressmen and senators to speed up the process availed nothing. The delay was neither deliberate nor purposeful. The Army's apparently slow and incremental pace, though highly frustrating at times, was carefully calculated to avoid errors and a rush to judgment. They undertook the task of evaluation and scrutiny with great care and precision.

The new year (1996) generated renewed interest, a flurry of activities, and some very good news. Through the grapevine, the author heard that seven of the ten cases submitted and recommended for reevaluation had been approved for the Medal of Honor by a special Army Awards Board. The board was made up of five men, and included at least two very senior officers, one of them a Medal of Honor recipient, as well as the highest ranking enlisted man in the Army. The board's task was to evaluate each case on its own merit and apply the criteria for qualification and approval of the Medal of Honor. The board took its task seriously and did it in a highly professional manner. Its decision to award the nation's highest medal for gallantry in combat to seven black soldiers was a clear vindication of the Army's changing policies and firm commitment to do what is right and just.

In early May another round of activities galvanized the Washington bureaucracy. Joseph Galloway, a military journalist with *U.S. News & World Report*, received a copy of the study and his endeavors set in motion a train of compelling events that would finally elicit an announcement from the White House.

Galloway had, some years before, become interested in efforts to obtain a Medal of Honor for Sergeant Reuben Rivers, a black tanker in General George Patton's Third Army, who had died heroically in action in Europe. He had, in the parlance of his trade, begun "saving string" on the question of medals of valor awarded to black American soldiers in combat. He was aware of the Shaw University study. What he did not know was that the study had been completed, the awards board recommendations made, and the whole process seemingly hung up for months pending action by President Clinton.

Two separate sources offered Galloway copies of the Shaw report, and with a copy in hand the reporter and his *U.S. News & World Report* colleagues set out to find the relatives of the nine black American heroes recommended in the report for posthumous medals, and to locate and interview Lieutenant Vernon J. Baker. This they did in less than one week, preparing a detailed account of the awards process and how it had pared the list down to seven Medals of Honor. The story ran on the May 6, 1996, cover of *U.S. News* under a huge red headline:

Military Injustice. It created renewed excitement nationwide and galvanized the political bureaucracy into action.

The White House confirmed details of the magazine's story and announced that President Clinton would approve the award of the Medal to the seven named individuals just as soon as Congress passed the enabling legislation. Baker and the family members of five of the six posthumous recipients told their stories and set off a frenzy of news coverage. No surviving kin of Private George Watson could be found, either by the media or by the Army Awards Board. His medal would eventually be accepted by a representative of the U.S. Army.

President Clinton's announcement ended all speculation and brought great relief to relatives and other concerned individuals and organizations. It was a time to celebrate; the long, agonizing wait was finally over. The author and other members of the research team looked forward to January 13, 1997, when the commander-in-chief would, by an act of Congress, change United States military history. In presenting the Medal of Honor to seven black World War II veterans, he brought closure to a long struggle and brought much healing in the African-American communities across this nation.

A President and the Medal

On January 13, 1977, a day that will forever be etched in the memory of African Americans, particularly black veterans of World War II and former members of the 92nd Infantry Division, United States military history was changed. No longer would the official record show that no African-American soldier received the nation's highest military decoration for valor in combat — the Medal of Honor — during World War II. Instead, it now shows that seven African-American soldiers who fought in World War II received the Medal of Honor.

The absence of a black recipient of the medal — carried for half a century — was finally changed on this day in January. On this cold, wintry day in the nation's capital, President Bill Clinton awarded seven black soldiers the Medal of Honor. Of the seven, only one recipient was alive — Vernon Baker — the other six medals were posthumous awards presented to families of the fallen heroes. This final segment of this brief history of the 92nd Infantry Division looks at the Medal of Honor and the ceremony that changed American military history.

The Medal of Honor

A U.S. Army study, first published in 1948, succinctly captures in simple language the quintessential point of the Medal of Honor award: "He who possesses the Medal of Honor is the recipient of the highest military award for bravery in combat that can be given to any individual in the United States of America."[2] During world wars I and II, the medal could be earned only one way — that was by a deed of personal bravery or self-sacrifice, above and beyond the call of duty, while a member of the American armed forces, and in actual combat against an enemy of the nation.

Army regulations permit no margin of error or doubt about the requirements. The deed of the recipient must be demonstrated by incontestable evidence of at least two eyewitnesses; it must be so outstanding that it clearly distinguishes his gallantry beyond the call of duty from lesser forms of bravery; it must involve the risk of his life; and it must be the type of deed which, if he had not done it, would not subject him to any justified criticism.[3]

As the highest-ranking and best-known United States decoration for heroism in combat, the Medal of Honor compares in prestige and precedent to the British Victoria Cross, an award that the British Army very seldom makes. Often mistakenly called the "Congressional Medal of Honor," "It is in fact awarded in the name of the Congress of the United States and, whenever possible, the President of the United States personally makes its presentation."[4]

For decades after its creation during the Civil War, there was an absence of a consistent set of policies or criteria for the award. Neither were there any clear-cut rules or procedures for documenting and validating the acts of gallantry befitting the decoration. Many commanders took advantage of their positions and exercised their own judgment and set their own standards for the medal. The situation was at best chaotic and at times ego driven. It had to be corrected and soon.

Faced with the need to regularize the procedures for the medal, Congress in 1916 approved an act that provided for the creation of a "Medal of Honor Roll" upon which honorably discharged medal recipients who had attained the age of 65 would be recorded. This act also created a Decorations Board whose task was to gather all Medal of Honor records, prepare statistics, classify cases and organize evidence that might be used in its deliberations. Over the course of three months, the board considered all of the 2,625 Medals of Honor that had been awarded up to that time.

On February 15, 1917, exactly one month after its period of deliberations ended, the board struck 911 cases off its official list. Of these 911 names, 864 were from a single regiment. The board felt that the Medal had not been properly awarded for distinguished services by the definition of the act of June 3, 1916. Although it had few legal definitions to guide it in its work, the board not only did a magnificent job of evaluation, but its action with respect to the 911 cases sent a clear message to Congress that greater legal clarification was needed.

Congress responded two years later in July 1918. The House passed an act that finally redefined the criteria for the medal and set forth precise rules for the award, saying in legislation that the recipient must "distinguish himself conspicuously by gallantry and intrepidity at the risk of life above and beyond the call of duty."[5] But apart from these considerations, the 1918 act also created for the first time in American history the notion of degrees of service to the country, each worthy of recognition, but only one of which could be accorded supreme recognition.

Guided by this new set of criteria during World War I, the Army awarded only 95 Medals of Honor at the end of this global conflict. It wanted to reserve the Medal for only those few acts of truly extraordinary heroism in battle. Through legislation, definition, administration, review of applications and recommendations was built up a solid base for the award of the Medal of Honor. When World War II struck, the Army seemed to be well prepared to administer a swift and accurate reward for many provable cases of extraordinary valor in combat.

A War Department Decorations Board was established during World War II, and in its review and evaluation of each case for the medal it was guided by two principles. The first was that failure to recognize true valor promptly would defeat the purpose of the decorations system. And the second was that to make an unmerited award for the Medal of Honor would depreciate the true value of the award to those who really deserved it. Cognizant of what the medal stood for in American history, the board in its effort to protect the integrity of the award exercises diligent care that only the truly deserving receive the decoration. Thus during World War II, the board was not only more keenly aware of the rules and regulations for the medal, but it was also guided by the same policy of parsimony (as in WWI) when it handed out only 294 medals during this war. Of that total, none was bestowed on a black soldier.

Herein lies the irony of the Army's decorations system — a system that was not rigorously enforced at the higher levels of command where senior commanders failed and in some instances refused to forward Medal of Honor recommendations to the board for final approval or disapproval. Only the Decorations Board, set up by the War Department, could approve or disapprove a Medal of Honor recommendation. In short, final authority rested with the Department of Defense and not with any individual commander, whatever his rank. Moreover, all recommendations for the medal, once initiated from the field, must be forwarded to the board and not kept back or discarded in the case of a disapproval.

Apart from World War II, in which there was no black recipient of the Medal of Honor, all other major U.S. military engagements in which black soldiers participated accounted for some. The following table, constructed from several sources, gives a breakdown of the list by campaigns:

Black Medal of Honor Recipients as of December 1996

Campaigns/Wars	Army	Navy	Marines
Civil War	16	7	0
Indian Campaigns	18	0	0
Spanish American War	5	1	0
World War I	1	0	0
World War II	0	0	0
Korean War	2	0	0
Vietnam War	15	0	5

But what exactly is the medal and what does it represent in American society? Answers to these questions are important, given the paucity of knowledge and high level of misunderstanding about the true nature of this medal. Designed by Christian Schussel and sculpted by Anthony Paquet in 1861, the Medal of Honor is not merely the five-pointed piece of engraved bronze metal suspended by a light blue ribbon and worn around the neck.

It is infinitely more than metal and molecules. It is a concept, an idea that goes beyond the Medal itself, beyond the deeds that are recorded, beyond the legislation that brought it into existence and redefined its criteria, and beyond the boards of review. These are the elements that make up the structure of protection of the medal and for the perpetuation of its ideals. And the concept that this structure supports remains something very difficult, if not impossible, of definition — simply because the medal is not a concrete or material thing.

The Medal of Honor is an ideal, an ideal that springs from the deepest roots of all that is the noblest and best in humanity. It embodies the American ideals of individual freedom and liberty, the big-hearted American spirit of gratitude, the spirit of the individual's quest for preeminence and unselfishness, and the democratic beliefs of a nation blessed by God.

This belief in liberty is what has and continues to fuel the spirit of national development and individual achievement in this country — a belief that is more important today than ever before. To preserve it in a world torn by strife and embittered by ethnic hatred and violent conflicts, it is necessary for all who believe in democracy and freedom to realize that they themselves constitute an army — and that their tasks are just as real as any that could be assigned on the battlefield.

The cause for which the American Army does its work is the same cause for which lovers of freedom have always struggled: the right to live one's life as one pleases, without fear of interference or coercion by others, and granting others the same freedom in return. For this kind of service, in this kind of army, there can be only one reward — the personal knowledge that one has done his best, rising above the din and confusion of petty squabbles, rising to a higher height in personal bravery and sacrifice, and in the process inspiring others to achieve greater heights. This in truth is the Medal of Honor, the "Blue Max," and it was for this kind of service — honoring those who have displayed such stupendous feats of courage under fire — that a special ceremony marking the occasion was held in the East Room at the White House on January 13, 1977.

The Ceremony

The attendees were a select group. Assembled in the East Room of the White House were men and women from all walks and stations of American life. Many came from far off places. Several were escorted by the United States military. In attendance were members of the president's cabinet, senior military brass, living recipients of the Medal of Honor, relatives and families of those who would be honored today, members of the media including the press and television, former chairman of the Joint Chiefs of Staff, General Colin Powell, Secretary of the Army Togo West, and his predecessor, Acting Secretary John Shannon were all there.

It was John Shannon who in 1990 breathed new life into a comatose idea when he set aside funds for a special study to find out why no black soldier received the Medal of Honor in World War II. This initiative would set in motion a train of events that finally culminated in the Army's decision to award seven African Americans the Medal of Honor. And it was Togo West, who as secretary of the army, made the important decision and instructed the Army Awards Branch to act on the study's recommendations and convene a special Awards Board for a case-by-case evaluation. The Army Awards Branch, after a thorough and painstaking assessment that lasted exactly two years, recommended that six black Distinguished Service Cross and one Silver Star recipients be upgraded to the Medal of Honor.

Gathered in this room also were the many friends and relatives of the seven recipients. Expectancy rested on their faces. They had heard of the bravery and acts of courage displayed by their loved ones before death snatched them away. For many years they waited; today the waiting was over. The author spoke to several of these family members. They were simple folks, many from rural America. But they all had a sense of what is right and wrong and they demonstrated no signs of bitterness. They were very appreciative of the work that had been undertaken to make this day and this event possible, and many openly expressed their gratitude.

For the Rivers and Carter families in particular, this day brought a settled peace and a feeling of great relief. It would close a long and painful chapter in their lives. These families had experienced tremendous agony; their hopes ebbed and flowed for over thirty years. Then there was also David Williams, the white company commander of Staff Sergeant Ruben Rivers. Indefatigable in his efforts and unrelenting in his tenacity, Captain Williams, now nearly eighty years old, had fought for recognition for Sergeant Rivers since the mid–1970s. He never wavered in his faith that justice would be done before his time was done. He spoke glowingly and passionately of Ruben Rivers. It was infectious. Today he was a special guest at the White House. His dream and search for justice had finally come true.

The East Room was packed, every available seat occupied. It was brightly lit with soft incandescent lights. To the front was a platform on which stood a lectern. And behind this lectern was a row of eight seats, one for each recipient of the medal and one for the President of the United States.

Family members and relatives were seated in the first four rows in the section right of the lectern. At the very center of the room were rows of seats reserved for cabinet ministers and military brass. The author and Professor Kohn sat together in the section opposite the family members. The general atmosphere was very subdued. Exchanges between and among acquaintances were kept low and hardly audible. Expectancy filled the air as we all waited with bated breath for the announcement. And then it came; the moment we had waited for.

A male voice, clear and resonant, arrested our attention: "Ladies and gentlemen, First Lieutenant Vernon Baker." A thunderous applause spontaneously erupted as every one stood and turned to the main aisle. All eyes strained to catch a glimpse of this hero. And there he was, the only living black recipient to be honored today, slowly making his way to the podium. Lt. Baker looked dignified and immaculate in his dark blue suit. His gait was steady and his form erect as he strode toward the podium. All eyes were fixed on him. The applause continued until he mounted the podium and faced the audience.

The voice continued with the roll call. As each designated family member made his or her way to the podium to receive the medal on behalf of their loved ones, there was a round of applause greeting each name. The seventh and last name that was announced came as a surprise. It was that of Army Sergeant Major Gene McKinney, the top noncommissioned officer in the U.S. Army, who would receive the medal on behalf of Private George Watson. No living relative of Watson was located in spite of several attempts by the Army and a *U.S. News & World Report* team that researched and ran a cover story on these heroes in its May 1996 issue. It was a sad moment. Watson was the first black soldier to receive the Distinguished Service Cross in World War II. And on this day when the nation's highest military award would be presented to him posthumously, there was no relative or family member present to receive it.

There followed a slightly longer pause after McKinney ascended the podium and faced the audience. "Ladies and gentlemen," the voice roared, "the President of the United States of America, William Jefferson Clinton." The audience, already on its feet, burst into a fresh round of applause, louder than before.

With his eyes fixed in the direction toward the podium and steps steady and deliberate, he walked slowly. He did not pause to shake hands or greet members of the audience. This was not a political meeting with rabid fans and die-hard supporters. Rather, this was a special occasion, a ceremony in which a grateful nation would finally honor seven of its bravest black soldiers. Every aspect of it must bear the stamp of dignity and solemnity, and President Clinton was just perfect in the role of commander-in-chief.

Following an invocation by Major General Donald W. Shea, Army chief of chaplains, the President stepped toward the lectern, standing in full view of the audience. The humming noise in the room immediately ceased, giving way to a short-lived deafening silence. Dressed in a navy blue suit and taking a quick look at the audience, he paused for just a few seconds before speaking. All ears were now strained to hear his every word. In a prepared speech that lasted well over twenty-five minutes, the President reminded this nation of the difficulties and hardships that blacks had to endure in this country fifty years ago. He said that in spite of racial discrimination, personal affront to their dignity, and relative deprivations, many blacks soldiered on with courage, defending everything noble that this country stood for. Today, he reminded us, the time has come in this nation's history when it must bury the injustices of the past and do the right thing for a group of men who fought as true Americans in World War II.

Digressing to share a light moment about Lieutenant Baker's recent encounter with a mountain lion that was now safe in his deep-freeze, the President expressed his appreciation to all those who made this occasion possible and thanked the research team for their study. This nation, the President said, has the capacity to take corrective action, to examine its past, and to go forward comfortable in the knowledge that it has done its duty to all its citizens. It was an impressive speech delivered in cadences of extraordinary pathos. Its emotional and patriotic appeal was truly captivating. Bill Clinton was at his best, causing everyone in that room to feel good about being an American. Because America, he said, stood for all that is noble, lofty, and good.

Following the President's speech, the awards ceremony began. A Marine officer standing behind a smaller lectern to the left of the podium read each citation. Vernon Baker was first in line to receive his medal. He along with the President and an officer aide stood while the citation was read. We listened with rapt attention as the story outlining his acts of courage unfolded.

There was no doubt in anyone's mind that Baker's gallantry on April 5, 1945, on Hill X in Italy deserved the Medal of Honor. Out came the medal suspended by a light blue ribbon. The President carefully placed it around Baker's neck. A handshake and a slight embrace followed. As the President said something to Baker still gripping his right hand in a handshake, the tears in Baker's eyes began to flow. This was an emotionally charged moment. The President himself was visibly shaken, fighting desperately to keep his composure. There was not a dry eye in that East Room.

Next to receive the medal was the niece of Major Charles Thomas, followed by the widow of Lieutenant John Fox, Mrs. Arlene Fox. A small woman, she was dwarfed by the President. Yet she did not flinch in his presence or before this assembly, but maintained a dignified composure. The medal was given to her and not placed around her neck. Only a live recipient would experience that. As each relative stood before the President to receive the medal from his hand, the marine officer read aloud the citation. This went on for several minutes with meticulous attention and due respect given to each case. The ceremony ended after Master Sergeant McKinney received the medal on behalf of Private George Watson.

The audience stood one last time as the President and other platform participants left the room. Following closely behind the commander-in-chief was Vernon Baker with his freshly minted medal hung around his neck. It looked resplendent, adding a luster to his stature and a modicum of dignity to his graceful strides. His exit from the East Room once again galvanized the media into action. They pursued him relentlessly. He was the star in today's show and he made the most of it. Justice, finally done. It was a great day in this nation's history.

7

SUMMARY AND CONCLUSION

This brief history of the 92nd Infantry Division during the course of the Ligurian Campaign in World War II is the story of an all-black unit preparing for and fighting a war under unfavorable physical and social conditions. It is also the story of human tragedy and triumph, of leadership characterized by a lack of foresight and compassion, of segregation based on racial discrimination — an idea nefarious in its conception and deleterious in its application — of bigotry, distrust, and hatred, and of tenacity and triumph of the human spirit. It is also a story of patience, patience born in adversity and characterized by endurance.

This history of the division also covers its activation and training before World War II, and it demonstrated that it is one of perseverance, of overcoming formidable obstacles, and of settling the persistent, yet recalcitrant question: do blacks make good combat soldiers? In the end, this short history would establish and confirm a salient and puissant fact that the fighting ability of troops is not a racial matter predicated on one's pigmentation. Rather, it is unquestionably a matter of training, of motivation and morale, and of leadership. It is also a matter of the will to fight, of courage and self-worth, and of the human spirit. When these ingredients are lacking in and among troops, the consequences and outcomes are predictable. The apparent failure of elements of the all-black 92nd Division to consistently engage the enemy and fight with grit and determination is traceable to four major conditions. A single factor or condition, however compelling, would clearly not suffice as an adequate explanation. And the reason for this is quite simple. Explanations of social phenomena do not come to us in a neat package of fixed laws and proofs. Rather, they are encrusted and sometimes buried, and must therefore be ferreted out and rigorously examined. In short, they are not single and isolated but multiple and complex. Following is a summary of these conditions:

- Segregation combined with apathy and distrust. The racial segregation of troops during World War II was at best operationally disastrous and an obloquy to an entire race of people. It created a climate of bigotry on the one hand and distrust and resentment on the other. As part of the Army's official policy, its rigid and vigorous implementation led to alienation and bitterness. It spawned and sustained a high level of distrust among troops, particularly between white commanders and their lower ranks of black officers and enlisted men. But while this reality pervaded the larger domestic social environment, its effects, particularly on the battlefield, were ominously destructive. Had senior white commanders treated blacks with respect and mitigated their own stance on segregation, the morale of their troops would have greatly improved and distrust almost receded. But such was not the case. The harsh, unyielding climate of strict racial segregation on the battlefield placed an extra burden on an already crumbling operational architecture. Distrust with its attendant implications did not surface overnight. It was an incremental, yet unavoidable reaction. And while this intractable problem could have been managed with more care and diligence, it was left unattended to ferment and escalate. Throughout the period of its training at Fort Huachuca and its sojourn in Italy, distrust was an ever-present state of affairs within the 92nd Infantry Division. When combined with strict racial segregation, failure in combat performance was an ineluctable consequence.

- Lack of motivation and low morale. This twin-blade problem cut deeply into the operational anatomy of the division. Under the overarching framework of segregation, its manifestation was real and pervasive throughout rank and file. It created a general feeling of malaise among troops culminating in the development of a pernicious attitude toward combat. From its early training period in the U.S., black members of the division shared a nascent belief that they were not getting ready for combat missions. It was a false, but highly disturbing rumor, and perceived otherwise, its effects were devastating to morale. The spread of wild and destructive rumors could have been dealt with or even checked had white leadership been more open and honest with their black troops. Their lack of sensitivity to genuine problems blacks faced on a quotidian basis and their reluctance to even address some of these problems aggravated an already depressing situation.

  This apparent lack of belief in the seriousness of their training quickly spread and fanned the flames of resentment and hatred. Motivation suffered under this climate resulting in an attitude of "just going through the motion." Cognizant of this problem and addressing it head on several years after the war ended, Ulysses Lee in his book, *The Employment of Negro Troops*, made the following observations: (1) a lack of belief in the personal integrity of [white] officers, (2) ignorance of the effects of language and action, (3) an inability by commanders to gauge the depths of morale problems, (4) ignorance of temper of command that is based primarily on insulation from enlisted men, and (5) excessive faith in the efficacy of hortatives.[1] In short, white commanders and their enlisted men had no common meeting ground, the chasm between them was never bridged and no real attempt was ever made on the part of leadership to do that. In the end, according to one historian, "Morale and motivation crumbled to the point that neither the routine of training and employment, the expansion of physical facilities, nor the hortatives of the well meaning had any significant effect."[2]

- Low levels of educational attainment. The employment of suitably qualified Negro manpower into the Armed Forces of the United States during World War II was a conspicuously arduous task. Compared with their white counterparts, Negroes lagged far behind in every social index including levels of education. So it was no surprise when large numbers were rejected for military service. And of those who were finally accepted, a large proportion barely crossed the line of acceptability. Thus the Army branch of the service that absorbed most of the Negro recruits also had the larger share of individuals who were at the lower levels of educational attainment. While this reality presented a formidable problem to begin with, it was compounded and exacerbated when large numbers of these individuals were placed in the same units. The end result, given a situation where inductees could barely read or write, let alone understand a field manual and navigate with a compass at night, was a questionable preparation for war. In the first place these men should not have been accepted into the Army. But having accepted them, measures aimed at dispersion should have been put in place. This very tactic was successfully utilized for whites whose education and test scores were at the lower levels. The Army's Band-Aid approach to alleviate the Negro problem fell short of success as many of these approaches were mechanical and not geared toward addressing the more substantial issues they faced. In short, low test scores and the generally poor social backgrounds of Negro recruits, while central to their military training and preparation for combat, were not exclusively or solely accountable for their subsequent performance on the battlefield.

- Leadership. At the heart of the explanation of the 92nd's poor combat performance in Italy lies segregation and leadership. While segregation was policy, leadership was not. The appointment of some senior white commanders, including that of Major General Edward Almond as division commander, as leaders of black troops was a recipe for failure. General Almond in particular held very strong racist views and, lock stitched into a conceptual straightjacket that treated blacks as servile and inferior, he was from the inception a bad choice for leadership. Apart from his racist views and orientation, Almond's questionable leadership ability and style were manifested in a number of other areas. He was aloof and austere, not in tune with his men. He consistently failed to recognize the extent of the morale problem the division was experiencing, and he showed very little interest in the welfare of the men he was leading. Moreover, his prior exposure to commanding black troops was negligible and his experiences as a commander were severely limited. As a tactician and strategist, he was poor and excessively egotistical. Many of the disasters that the division experienced in Italy were directly attributable to him. In this regard, his inflated ego would not allow him to take responsibilities for failure, but to place it directly on the men he was leading. Additionally, Almond's failure to recognize acts of heroism by individual blacks was unconscionable and an abdication of responsible leadership. It is not an overstatement of fact to say that leadership, and his leadership in particular, was mainly responsible for the division's numerous failed attempts to engage the enemy and hold their ground in Italy.

Given its relatively simple tasks during the war, the 92nd Infantry Division performance in combat was characterized in the main by failure yet punctuated by individual acts of heroism. A unit, plagued by myriad internal problems since its inception, well trained but poorly led, was nevertheless in high spirits on the eve of its departure to the war zone. During the course of its operations in the rugged mountains and treacherous valleys and river crossings in Italy, its performance raised significant questions about the combat suitability of Negroes. But while on the one hand this plethora of questions was legitimate, their answers on the other hand were remarkable for a paucity of adequate analysis. To lay the blame for failure squarely on enlisted men and junior officers, in short, on Negroes and their shortcomings as a race, and not on leadership and other significant factors, would indeed be shortsighted and irresponsible.

This brief history of the all-black 92nd Infantry Division has attempted to place in proper perspective those conditions and factors responsible for its combat failure in Italy, and to spotlight the display of heroism of two of its black soldiers. The events chronicled here are selective and in no way constitutes a comprehensive history of the division. Yet the accounts shed light on a darker side of war and of America going to and fighting a war. The award of two Medals of Honor, the nation's highest award for gallantry in combat, to two of the division's black men, is final vindication to veterans of the division that they fought bravely and performed well in the Ligurian Campaign. The bestowal of those awards also revealed America's capacity to correct acts of injustices and follow a right course of action.

It is hard to believe that less than fifty years ago black Americans were sent into combat, in Korea, in rigidly segregated units commanded by white officers. And it is equally hard to believe that the white military establishment adhered to the view that black soldiers were still unfit to serve in combat. That they lacked aggression in battle and were unreliable as infantrymen was clearly not an otiose sentiment but a strongly held belief. When a colleague of the author interviewed a senior white military officer, now retired, and expressed his amazement at the way the Army treated its black soldiers during the first half of the 20th century, he responded truthfully: "You have to remember that back then we were all racists; all of white America, North and South alike."[3]

One reason that this is so hard to believe now is because of the manpower makeup of today's American military. More than 30 percent of the Army's soldiers are blacks. The American military, after so terrible a beginning, blatantly racial and unflinchingly draconian in some of its policies, has become for black Americans one of the most level of playing fields in this nation. This transformation attests to the capacity of white Americans to make amends and rise to a higher level of human dignity and decency. The American Army today is a proud fighting force representing all of its different peoples. If you can do the job, if you can meet the stated standards, you have a future and a career in the Army, the Navy, the Marine Corps, and the Air Force. Color is no bar. Once a formidable and recalcitrant problem, it is no longer an issue that warrants serious debate. Black soldiers watched with pride as one of their own, General Colin Powell, served a brilliant tour as chairman of the Joint Chiefs of Staff, the nation's highest military post. It was the first time that a black would be appointed to this position, an appointment inconceivable fifty years ago. Black soldiers fought bravely and well in Vietnam, in Grenada, in Panama, in the Persian Gulf War, and have served valiantly in the dozens of peace-keeping missions mounted since then in Somalia and Bosnia and Kosovo.

We owe our respect and salute to those black American pioneers who not only volunteered to serve in World War II, but who actually had to mount a political campaign to persuade white America to send them off to fight and die overseas for their country. Their numbers, like those of their white counterparts, are dwindling rapidly. Today, fewer than one hundred veterans of the 92nd Infantry Division turn up for their annual reunion in Washington, D.C. And we owe it also to Vernon Baker and John Fox and all those brave black heroes who fought with courage in World War II.

8

Epilogue: An Encounter with America

It was an awe-inspiring and emotionally uplifting occasion, sublime in its purpose and stentorian in its historic significance. It was free from the encroachments and bickering of partisan politics and dignified by a national spirit of gratitude. The President of this great democracy was about to recognize and bestow upon seven African-American soldiers who fought in World War II the nation's highest honor for gallantry in combat, the Medal of Honor.

It was an unusual occasion in more ways than one. For rarely in the military history of this country had such a far-reaching and significant decision been made, a decision to correct a grave act of injustice against men who suffered the intolerable indignities of racial discrimination in a society that espoused the belief that all men are created equal. These men, like most of their comrades who served in this nation's armed forces during the war, not only endured severe hardships and mistreatment at the hands of white commanders on and off the battlefield, but also fought bravely and courageously despite their heinous treatment. Two of these heroes to be honored on this solemn occasion were from the 92nd Infantry Division. One survived to recount his saga; the other never made it back to his homeland alive.

It was also a strange occasion for me personally — a non–American at the time, there I was at the White House, one of the many invited guests to witness this solemn, dignified, and historic ceremony. I had never seen anything like it before, and the experience of being there, knowing that I had had a hand in the unfolding drama, was exhilarating and deeply satisfying.

In this epilogue I would like to tell my story — to describe the experiences that evolved into an encounter with America. It was an encounter that truly transformed my own outlook and thinking about America and about African Americans.

In early July 1991, I left my family in Barbados, where my wife worked as an economist at the Caribbean Development Bank for North Carolina, to take up my first real job after completing a British doctorate a year earlier. It was a momentous journey filled with emotions and anxieties. The pain of leaving my wonderful wife and two small children tugged at my heartstrings.

I was also anxious about the new job, not having been educated in the United States and having little knowledge of American academia. I had gotten accustomed to the rigor of British academic style and substance and felt comfortable in its ways. What little understanding I had of American learning and teaching styles came largely from bits and pieces garnered in conversations with Americans I had met earlier. Many of these were students who took graduate classes with me in Sweden and England. They were a young and enterprising lot, those Americans, several with a proclivity for adventure and sightseeing.

And so with anxious foreboding I came to Shaw University in Raleigh, North Carolina, on a hot summer's day in July.

A small campus sandwiched between North Carolina State University to the north and St. Augustine College to the south, Shaw University, a private Baptist-affiliated school of higher education, was one of the earliest academic institutions established for the education of African Americans. It boasted a long and rich history. When free blacks sought higher education in this country and were denied entrance to majority white institutions, many turned to Shaw, where they found not only refuge, but also a center of learning. Shaw became in those early days a magnet for black students, attracting those who could and couldn't afford an education. True to its mission, its doors were opened to all who diligently sought academic enrichment and career development. Little did I realize then that I had come to such a culturally rich and historically significant academic institution.

At the end of my second year, while preparing to attend the United States Military Academy at West Point to learn the Army's way of teaching military history, I responded to a request for proposal from the Department of Defense. I soon learned that under constant political pressure from varied interest groups, particularly the veterans of the 92nd Infantry Division, the then acting secretary of the Army, John Shannon, had finally ordered that a special archival study be undertaken to determine whether there might be one or possibly more unprocessed recommendations for the Medal of Honor for black soldiers who fought in World War II. It was an audacious and wise move—fiercely resisted by Shannon's predecessors—that would finally bring closure to a long, sustained struggle. Shannon's directive was but one in a series of positive moves that would eventually culminate in the award of seven Medals of Honor to black veterans of World War II.

Preparing the proposal for the Department of Defense request was a major undertaking for me. Fortuitously, I had met Richard Kohn from UNC–Chapel Hill a few months before. Professor Kohn is not only an eminent military historian but also a warm and very friendly gentleman. His assistance to me and to the effort was invaluable in a number of important ways, ranging from the recruitment of historians for the team to answering technical questions and overhauling the written proposal. If there is one individual who, above all others, was singularly responsible for shaping and making my American encounter a pleasant and meaningful reality, that individual was unquestionably Richard Kohn.

Towards the end of September 1993, the contract award from the Department of Defense arrived. Emotions ran high. I even hugged Dr. Talbert Shaw, the president of Shaw University, when I shared the good news with him. Contacting other members of the research team at their homes, and the chief contracting officer at the Army Awards Branch, we arranged within days our first meeting in Alexandria, Virginia.

Throughout the proposal phase, I had spoken with Drs. Elliott Converse and Robert Griffith, members of the research team, on the phone several times, but had never seen them in person. I had already met the other researcher whom Kohn had initially recommended, Col. John Cash, an African-American military historian.

The meeting was eventful. The contracting officer showed much enthusiasm for the project and reiterated many times the precise nature of the undertaking. The team's major tasks were to comb the archives thoroughly in order to identify the names of all black soldiers recommended for the Medal of Honor; to verify that the procedures used in processing the recommendations met the standards set by public law and the War Department; to identify unprocessed recommendations; and to document breaches in the handling of those unprocessed recommendations. It was a major undertaking, but the team was up to it.

Six months into the research effort, with hundreds of hours spent poring over archival materials at several repositories (including the National Archives then located at Suitland, Maryland, and the US Army Military History Institute at Carlisle Barracks, Pennsylvania), the team excavated but one Medal of Honor recommendation for an officer of the 92nd Infantry Division. We were jubilant, but the euphoria was short-lived. It turned out that this officer was white. The officer, Captain John Runyon, was recommended by a Gen. Wood for the Medal of Honor for actions on April 5, 1945, but said recommendation was disapproved by the Mediterranean Theater Headquarters and then forwarded to the War Department in Washington, D.C., where it met the same fate. It turned out that Captain Runyon had once served as Gen. Wood's aide before becoming a company commander in the 92nd Division. At the end of this halfway point milestone on the archival dig and with no real prospect in sight for unearthing a recommendation for a black soldier, a spirit of uneasiness developed, quickly giving rise to exasperation. But all was not lost.

At this juncture, Kohn and I attended an important meeting at the Army Awards Branch with the contracting officer and the colonel in charge of the project. After hearing our report the colonel was forthright in her conclusion: Bring the study to a close and submit your final report. We were devastated, unwilling to concede that the effort could be truncated so early. I could not believe what I was hearing. The colonel based her decision on the fact that our research effort had failed to unearth any unprocessed recommendation for the Medal for a black World War II veteran. The idea of continuing the effort seemed futile on her part.

Kohn requested more research time. I argued for a different approach. In the end, it did not matter. Her mind was made up. We walked out of that building with heads down, overcome by a feeling of disappointment. In the parking lot Kohn turned to me and said, "Dan, I told you that nothing would come out of this. It's too political. You are too naïve." I had no answer.

During the early phase of the project, Col. John Cash accompanied me on several interview trips. We met and interviewed a number of black veterans, including Lt. Vernon Baker and the late Hondon Hargrove. During some of these visits I encountered a level of reception that could only be described as hostile. The venom came from a number of African Americans who, when they saw that I was not an African American, immediately adopted a very unfriendly attitude. Several vented their frustrations towards the Department of Defense, using forceful invectives.

I sensed that there was a level of deep distrust among many of them — and for very good reasons, too. They had waited so long for some meaningful outcome, and they perceived that this venture was another "token" project by the establishment.

Col. Cash always saved the day. During these hostile encounters, he would take time to explain why in his opinion a non–African-American principal investigator would be fair and unbiased, and why this time the Department of Defense meant business. He unruffled many feathers and exuded a level of confidence that eventually won their trust.

Our meeting with and interview of Vernon Baker was the single most exciting event during the research phase of this project. Having read about Baker's acts of valor on the battlefield, I had developed in my mind an image of someone tall and powerfully built, a mean killing machine. But here he was before us, a five feet eight inches tall and about 150 pounds, a quiet, and soft-spoken man, confident in his demeanor and very polite in his manner. During the course of our two-hour long interview, we were impressed by the clarity of his memory and the sharpness of his mind. He recalled the incident of April 5, 1945, as if it had happened a few days before. The description of the firefight and the sequence of events astounded us. In a very methodological way he walked us through the day's events, recalling with precision what he had written in a report forty-nine years earlier. Baker did not have a copy of his report and when we gave him one, he was overwhelmed.

Our final question to him was why he fought with such courage and determination, given the grinding hardships of segregation he and his comrades experienced. He answered simply, "I did it for my men," and then broke down in tears. His German-born wife, Heidi, who accompanied him and listened patiently to her husband's saga, was emotionally drained. It was a poignant moment for all of us. Col. Cash and I came away highly satisfied and feeling very confident that Vernon Baker is a true American hero.

Another individual who we were fortunate to interview and who elucidated with clarity the War Department's policy towards blacks during World War II was Truman Gibson. As civilian-aide to the secretary of war, Gibson was close to policy making and several important actors. It was clear that he understood the dynamic subtleties of racist propensities and manifestations prevalent at the time in the U.S. military. Gibson was a trusted aide who was relied upon for his insights and views on matters relating to blacks in the military. His briefs were noted for their clarity and force of argument. Moreover, he had undertaken a number of field trips observing living and training conditions under which black soldiers served. So he had a real and obvious sense of what these soldiers experienced under segregation.

We interviewed Gibson in his high-rise apartment in Chicago on March 12, 1994. I was somewhat bewildered when the apartment door opened and there stood a noble gentleman who to me looked "white." I was expecting to see a black person. Sensing my slight confusion he calmly said, "Hi, I am Truman Gibson, please to meet you." Col. Cash meanwhile was having a fit of a laughter.

Gibson was a gracious host. He answered our questions very succinctly, displaying the insights of an insider. When asked why the 92nd Infantry Division performed so badly in Italy, he answered, "The division was programmed to fail from the inception." Col. Cash looked at me and smiled. I understood immediately. We had heard this line before but were not convinced. But hearing it first hand from Gibson made a difference to us.

We also inquired about racism in the military during World War II. On this issue he had a lot to say. Racism and racial segregation in the Army, he asserted, was official policy. The Army, he believed, did not want to deviate from this policy and was not willing to take the lead in social experimentation. Gibson's experience and first hand knowledge was extremely useful and provided for us greater insights into the denouement of Army's policy and practices.

Back on the research trail two weeks after Kohn and I met with the contracting officer, I set out for the George Marshall Library in Lexington, Virginia. Located on the campus of Virginia Military Academy, the George Marshall Library houses not only the papers of General Marshall, but also important documentation pertaining to World War II. On my second day at this repository, I came across a copy of an out of print book titled *The Medal of Honor of the United States Army*. I painstakingly photocopied the entire book. That night in my hotel room I devoured its contents and was elated when I discovered that a precedent had been set in World War I by General J.J. Pershing to reevaluate and upgrade Distinguished Service Cross cases to the Medal of Honor.

It was an important discovery. Dr. Converse had earlier shared with us the contents of a letter written by General Eisenhower requesting that DSC cases in the Mediterranean Theater of Operations be reevaluated for possible upgrade to the Medal. Both exercises resulted in Medal of Honor awards to DSC recipients. There were now two compelling precedents. Why could the Army Awards Branch not do the same for black DSC recipients?

Using this latest find, we made a persuasive argument to the Army and finally won an extension of the contract (from twelve to fifteen months) and a change of research strategy. We were emboldened by this new development and set out with alacrity to accomplish the new tasks before us. Dr. Converse spearheaded the research effort at the National Archives and did a masterful job. By the end of December, the team's efforts had paid off handsomely. We were all pleased with the finished product, its quality, style, and academic rigor. It even exceeded the Army's expectations.

Shortly after this juncture, I received a call from the contractor representative telling me that the colonel had suddenly decided to go on early retirement. I breathed a prayer, which happily was answered. The new officer in charge, a major, was keen on the idea of going all the way up the chain of command with our approach and recommendations. He was responsible for breathing new life into the project, determined that something positive should come out of our effort. We found in him a keen listener and saw him as someone who was willing to step out of the military black box.

In early January 1995, I drove up to Alexandria, Virginia, and delivered six copies of the study to the contracting officer representative. It was a sunny but cold day. I was on an important mission, conscious of the fact that I had in my possession a research study that hopefully would change an aspect of American military history. I was also confident that the Army would not treat this study lightly and would take the necessary actions.

Throughout my sojourn during this three-year period, from the award of the contract in late September 1993 to the ceremony at the White House in mid–January 1997, I had the privilege of meeting and interacting with a wide cross section of Americans. I learned much about the collective history of African Americans—what they had suffered at the hands of their fellow citizens and what, despite their suffering, they had freely contributed to American society.

I also came to understand and appreciate the Medal of Honor and its exalted place in American military history. The medal represents all that is noble and good in this nation. There is nothing else like it. Americans are a pragmatic people whose love for freedom and individual effort are boundless. They are a people of remarkable ingenuity who share a common belief that the American way of life is unique and that Americans as a people have a strong and abiding faith in the rule of law and justice.

Indeed, my American encounter was an enlightening experience, an encounter that has reshaped my worldview, instilling in me the virtues of a noble and enlightened society.

Appendix: More Information on the Medal of Honor

Criteria for the Award

The Medal of Honor, established by Joint Resolution of Congress 12 July 1862 (amended by Act of 9 July 1918 and Act of 25 July 1963) is awarded in the name of Congress to a person who, while a member of the Armed Forces, distinguishes himself conspicuously by gallantry and intrepidity at the risk of his life above and beyond the call of duty while engaged in an action against any enemy of the United States, while engaged in military operations involving conflict with an opposing foreign force; or while serving with friendly forces engaged in an armed conflict against an opposing armed force in which the United States is not a belligerent party. The deed performed must have been one of personal bravery or self-sacrifice so conspicuous as to clearly distinguish the individual above his comrades and must have involved risk of life. Incontestable proof of the performance of service is exacted and each recommendation for award of this decoration is considered on the standard of extraordinary merit. Eligibility is limited to members of the Armed Forces of the United States in active Federal military service.

Citations

The President of the United States of America, authorized by Act of Congress, March 3, 1863, has awarded in the name of The Congress the Medal of Honor to

FIRST LIEUTENANT VERNON J. BAKER
UNITED STATES ARMY

For conspicuous gallantry and intrepidity at the risk of his life above and beyond the call of duty:

First Lieutenant Vernon J. Baker distinguished himself by extraordinary heroism in action on 5 and 6 April 1945. At 0500 hours on 5 April 1945, Lieutenant Baker advanced at the head of his weapons platoon, along with Company C's three rifle platoons, toward their objective; Caste Aghinolfi—a German mountain strong point on the high ground just east of the coastal highway and about two miles from the 370th Infantry Regiment's line of departure. Moving more rapidly than the rest of the company, Lieutenant Baker and about 25 men reached the south side of a draw some 250 yards from the castle within two hours. In reconnoitering for a suitable position to set up a machine gun, Lieutenant Baker observed two cylindrical objects pointing out of a slit in a mount at the edge of a hill. Crawling up and under the opening, he stuck his M-1 into the slit and emptied the clip, killing the observation post's two occupants. Moving to another position in the same area, Lieutenant Baker stumbled upon a well-camouflaged machine gun nest, the crew of which was eating breakfast. He shot and killed both enemy soldiers. After Captain John F. Runyon, Company C Commander, joined the group, a German soldier appeared from the draw and hurled a grenade which failed to explode. Lieutenant Baker shot the enemy soldier twice as he tried to flee. Lieutenant Baker then went down into the draw alone. There he blasted open the concealed entrance of another dugout with a hand grenade, shot one German soldier who emerged after the explosion, tossed another grenade into the dugout and entered firing his sub-machine gun, killing two more Germans. As Lieutenant Baker climbed back out of the draw, enemy machine gun and mortar fire began to inflict heavy casualties among the group of 25 soldiers, killing or wounding two-thirds of them. When expected reinforcements did not arrive, Captain Runyon ordered a withdrawal in two groups. Lieutenant Baker volunteered to cover the withdrawal of the first group, which consisted of mostly walking wounded, and to remain to assist in the evacuation of the more seriously wounded. During the second group's withdrawal, Lieutenant Baker, supported by covering fire from one of his platoon members, destroyed two machine gun positions (previously bypassed during the assault) with hand grenades. In all, Lieutenant Baker accounted for nine enemy dead soldiers, elimination of three machine gun positions, an observation post, and a dugout. On the following night, Lieutenant Baker voluntarily led a battalion advance through enemy mine fields and heavy fire toward the division objective. Lieutenant Baker's fighting spirit and daring leadership were an inspiration to his men and exemplify the highest traditions of the military service.

The President of the United States of America, authorized by Act of Congress, March 3, 1863, has awarded in the name of The Congress the Medal of Honor to

FIRST LIEUTENANT JOHN R. FOX
UNITED STATES ARMY

For conspicuous gallantry and intrepidity at the risk of his life above and beyond the call of duty:

First Lieutenant John R. Fox distinguished himself by extraordinary heroism at the risk of his own life on 26 December 1944 in the Serchio River Valley Sector, in the vicinity of Sommocolonia, Italy. Lieutenant Fox was a member of Cannon Company, 366th Infantry, 92nd Infantry Division, acting as a forward observer, while attached to the 598th Field Artillery Battalion. Christmas day in the Serchio Valley was spent in positions which had been occupied for some weeks. During Christmas night, there was a gradual influx of enemy soldiers in civilian clothes and by early morning the town was largely in enemy hands. An organized attack by uniformed German formations was launched around 0400 hours, 26 December 1944. Reports were received that the area was being heavily shelled by everything the Germans had, and although most of the U.S. infantry forces withdrew from the town, Lieutenant Fox and members of his observer party remained behind on the second floor of a house, directing defensive fires. Lieutenant Fox reported at 0800 hours that the Germans were in the streets and attacking in strength. He called for artillery fire increasingly close to his own position. He told his battalion commander, "That was just where I wanted it. Bring it in 60 yards." His commander protested that there was a heavy barrage in the area and the bombardment would be too close. Lieutenant Fox gave his adjustment, requesting that the barrage be fired. The distance was cut in half. The Germans continued to press forward in large numbers, surrounding the position. Lieutenant Fox again called for artillery fire with the commander protesting again, stating, "Fox, that will be on you!" The last communication from Lieutenant Fox was, "Fire it! There's more of them than there are of us. Give them hell!" The bodies of Lieutenant Fox and his party were found in the vicinity of his position when his position was taken. This action, by Lieutenant Fox, at the cost of his own life, inflicted heavy casualties, causing the deaths of approximately 100 German soldiers, thereby delaying the advance of the enemy until infantry and artillery units could be reorganized to meet the attack. Lieutenant Fox's extraordinarily valorous actions exemplify the highest traditions of the military service.

Black Recipients of the Medal of Honor, 1861–2000

Civil War (1861–1865)

William H. Carney, USA
Aaron Anderson, USN
William H. Barnes, USA
Powhatan Beaty, USA
Robert Blake, USN
James H. Bronson, USA
William H. Brown, USN
Wilson Brown, USN
Decatur Dorsey, USA
Christian Fleetwood, USA
James Gardiner, USA
James H. Harris, USA
Thomas R. Hawkins, USA
Alfred B. Hilton, USA
Milton Holland, USA
Alexander Kelly, USA
John Lawson, USN

Frontier War (1866–1890)

Emanual Stance, USA
Thomas Boyne, USA
Benjamin Brown, USA
John Denny, USA
Pompey Factor, USA
Clinton Greaves, USA
Henry Johnson, USA
Geogre Jordan, USA
William McBryar, USA
Isaiah Mays, USA
Adam Paine, USA
Isaac Payne, USA
Thomas Shaw, USA
Augustus Walley, USA
John Ward, USA
Moses Williams, USA
William O. Wilson, USA
Brent Woods, USA

Interim Period (1866–1898)

John Davis, USN
Alphonse Girandy, USN
John Johnson, USN
William Johnson, USN
Joseph B. Noil, USN
John Smith, USN
Robert Sweeney, USN

Spanish-American War (1898–1899)

Edward L. Baker, Jr., USA
Dennis Bell, USA
Fitz Lee, USA
Robert Penn, USN
William H. Thompkins, USA
George H. Wanton, USA

World War I
(1914–1918)

Freddie Stowers, USA

World War II
(1939–1945)

Vernon J. Baker, USA
Edward A. Carter, Jr., USA
John R. Fox, USA
Willy F. James, USA
Ruben Rivers, USA
Charles Thomas, USA
George Watson, USA

Korean War
(1950–1953)

Cornelius H. Charlton, USA
William Thomson, USA

Vietnam War
(1960–1973)

James Anderson, Jr., USMC
Webster Anderson, USA
Eugene Ashley, USA
Oscar P. Austin, USMC
William M. Bryant, USA
Rodney M. Davis, USMC
Robert H. Jenkins, Jr., USMC
Lawrence Joel, USA
Dwight H. Johnson, USA
Ralph H. Johnson, USMC
Garfield M. Langhorn, USA
Matthew Leonard, USA
Donald R. Long, USA
Milton L. Olive, III, USA
Riley L. Pitts, USA
Charles C. Rodgers, USA
Ruppert L. Sargeant, USA
Clarence E. Sasser, USA
Clifford C. Sims, USA
John E. Warren, Jr., USA

NOTES

Introduction

1. Maj. Gen. Robert L. Bullard, *Personalities and Reminiscences of the War* (New York: Doubleday, 1925), p. 298.
2. Henry Stimson and McGeorge Bundy, *On Active Service in Peace and War* (New York: Harper Brothers, 1947), p. 464.
3. Interview of Truman K. Gibson by Daniel Gibran at his home in Chicago, 1 March 1994, Chicago, IL.
4. General Edward Almond, "Approving Action of... Proceedings of Board of Review," 2 July 1945. General Almond Papers, U.S. Army Military History Institute, Carlisle Barracks, PA.

Chapter 1

1. Major Paul Goodman, *A Fragment of Victory: A Special Study Concerned with the 92d Infantry Division During World War II* (Carlisle Barracks, PA: Army War College, 1952), p. 1.
2. *Command of Negro Troops*, War Department Pamphlet, No. 20-6, 29 February 1944.
3. General Edward Almond, "Notes on an Evaluation of the Efficiency of the Negro in Military Operations Involving Combat," *Almond Papers*, (Carlisle Barracks, PA: U.S. Military History Institute, 1945), p. 6a.

4. Captain Thomas Fergusson, Interview with General Edward M. Almond, Anniston, Alabama, 26 March 1975.

5. Interview of Lt. Gen. William J. McCaffrey by Joseph Galloway, 29 January 1997, Alexandria, VA.

6. Ulysses Lee, *The Employment of Negro Troops*, Center for Military History, United States Army (Washington, D.C.: 1990), p. 266.

7. *Ibid.*, p. 300.

8. Brig. Gen. Benjamin O. Davis, *Memo for Inspector General*, 7 August 1943, General Davis Papers, Military History Institute, Carlisle Barracks, PA.

9. Maj. Gen. Edward Almond, "Notes on an Evaluation of the Efficiency of the Negro in Military Operations Involving Combat."

10. Morris MacGregor, *Integration of the Armed Forces 1940–1965* (Washington, D.C.: Center of Military History, 1989), p. 8.

11. Hondon Hargrove, *Buffalo Soldiers in Italy: Black Americans in World War II* (Jefferson, NC: McFarland, 1985), pp. 7–8.

12. *Ibid.*, p. 8.

13. Interview of Truman K. Gibson by Daniel K. Gibran, 12 March 1994, Chicago, IL.

14. Interview of Parren Mitchell by Col. John A. Cash, 1 March 1994, Washington, D.C.

15. Lee, *Employment of Negro Troops*, p. 334.

16. *Ibid.*, p. 295.

17. *Ibid.*, pp. 553–554.

18. Anonymous Letter to Lieutenant Bert Cumby, 23 February 1945, folder "Correspondence Regarding Personnel and Sundry Papers, April 1943–June 1945," Box 13620B, 92nd Infantry Division, World War II Operations Reports, 1940–1948, Record Group 407, Washington National Records Center.

19. Quoted in Lee, *Employment of Negro Troops*, p. 334.

20. Truman K. Gibson, Letter to Major General O.L. Nelson, Deputy Commander, Mediterranean Theater of Operations, "Report on Visit to 92nd Division," 12 March 1945, *Almond Papers* (United States Army Military History Institute, Carlisle Barracks, PA).

21. Hargrove, *Buffalo Soldiers in Italy*, p. 9.

22. *Ibid.*, p. 8.

23. Interview with General Edward Almond by Captain Thomas Fergusson, 25 March 1975, Anniston, AL.

24. *Ibid.*

25. *Ibid.*

26. *Ibid.*

27. *Ibid.*

28. Interview with General Edward Almond by Captain Thomas Fergusson, 26 March 1975, Anniston, AL.
29. *Ibid.*
30. *Ibid.*
31. *Ibid.*
32. Interview of Lt. Gen. William J. McCaffrey by Joseph Galloway, 29 January 1997, Alexandria, VA.
33. General Edward Almond's Notes on "The Utilization of Negro Manpower in the Army," 4 June 1959, Almond Papers, U.S. Army Military History Institute, Carlisle Barracks, PA.
34. Lee, *Employment of Negro Troops*, p. 550.

Chapter 2

1. Interview of Major General Edward Almond by Captain Thomas Fergusson, on 27 March 1975, Anniston, AL.
2. *Ibid.*
3. Hondon Hargrove, *Buffalo Soldiers in Italy: Black Americans in World War II* (Jefferson, NC: McFarland, 1985), p. 12.
4. See Paul Goodman, *A Fragment of Victory: The 92nd Infantry Division in Italy During World War II* (Carlisle Barracks, PA: Army War College, 1952), p. 21.
5. Goodman, *A Fragment of Victory*, p. 21.
6. "Eighth Army Drives for Po, Pisa Falls," *New York Times*, 2 September 1944, p. 10, sec. 1.
7. See Ulysses Lee, *The Employment of Negro Troops* (Washington, D.C.: United States Army, Center of Military History, 1990), p. 543.
8. Hargrove, *Buffalo Soldiers in Italy*, p. 25.
9. Lee, *The Employment of Negro Troops*, p. 543.
10. Goodman, *A Fragment of Victory*, p. 15.
11. Edward Gibbon, *Decline and Fall of the Roman Empire*, ed. by J.B. Bury, 2nd ed., vol. 4 (London: J. Murray Publishers, 1909), pp. 173–174.
12. Lee, *The Employment of Negro Troops*, p. 547.
13. *Ibid.*, pp. 548–49.
14. Statement of Lt. Robert D. Montjoy, Commander of Company C, 370th Infantry, 92nd Infantry Division, 15 October 1944, 92nd Infantry Division Files, National Archives, Suitland, MD.
15. *The Employment of Negro Troops*, p. 549.
16. Report of the Executive Officer, 370th Infantry Regiment, to Commander, 92nd Infantry Division, 13 October 1944, 92nd Division Files, National Archives, Suitland, MD.

17. Goodman, *A Fragment of Victory*, p. 105.
18. General Edward Almond, Letter to Commanding General, Fifth Army: Air Bombardment, Coastal Guns, 31 March 1945, Almond's Papers, Military History Institute, Carlisle Barracks, PA.
19. *Ibid*.
20. First Lieutenant Dennette Harrod, "Response to Questionnaire," 6 May 1980 (as quoted in Hargrove, *Buffalo Soldiers in Italy*, p. 99).
21. Interview of General Edward Almond by Captain Thomas Fergusson, 27 March 1975, Anniston, AL.
22. Major General Edward Almond, Letter to Lieutenant General Lucian Truscott, 11 February 1945, folder "Top Secret 92nd Infantry Division Combat Efficiency Analysis... ," Lee, *Employment of Negro Troops*, pp. 568–572.
23. Hondon Hargrove, *Buffalo Soldiers in Italy*, p. 145.
24. Interview of General Almond by Captain Thomas Fergusson, 27 March 1975, Anniston, AL.
25. Major General Edward Almond, Letter to Commanding General, Fifth Army, 18 February 1945, 92nd Infantry Division Files, National Archives, Suitland, MD.
26. Lee, *Employment of Negro Troops*, p. 575.
27. Interview of General William McCaffrey by Joseph Galloway, 29 January 1997, Alexandria, VA.
28. General Edward Almond, "Notes on an Evaluation of the Efficiency of the Negro in Military Operations Involving Combat," July 1945, Almond Papers, U.S. Army Military History Institute, Carlisle, PA.
29. *Ibid*.

Chapter 3

1. See Paul Goodman's, *A Fragment of Victory* (Carlisle Barracks, PA: Army War College, 1952), p. 125.
2. Captain John Runyon, Memorandum to Commanding General, 1 July 1945, "Report on Company C, 370th Infantry Regiment 5–6 April 1945," folder "Top Secret 92nd Infantry Division Combat Efficiency Analysis...." National Archives, Suitland, MD.
3. First Lieutenant Vernon Baker Report for Commanding General, 92nd Infantry Division, "Narrative of Action, 5 April 1945," 12 June 1945, folder "Top Secret 92nd Infantry Division Combat Efficiency Analysis...." National Archives, Suitland, MD.
4. Captain John Runyon, Memorandum to Commanding General.

5. *Ibid.*
6. Interview of Vernon Baker by Joseph Galloway and Daniel Gibran on 18 August 1996 at his home in St. Maries, ID.
7. *Ibid.*

Chapter 4

1. Interview of Vernon Baker by Joseph Galloway and Daniel Gibran on 28 August 1996 at his home in St. Maries, ID.
2. *Ibid.*
3. *Ibid.*
4. See General Joseph McNarney, Letter to Chief of Staff, 13 August 1945, attaching Headquarters, Mediterranean Theater of Operations report, "Participation of Negro Troops in the Post-War Military Establishment," 13 August 1945, folder "Army Ground Forces Report on Negro Troops," Box 183, Decimal 291.2, Army Ground Forces General Correspondence, 1942–1948, Record Group 337, National Archives, Suitland, MD.
5. Elliott Converse, Daniel Gibran, et al., *The Medal of Honor and African Americans in the United States Army During World War II*, An Archival Research Study Presented to the U.S. Army Military Awards Branch, Arlington, VA, January 1995, p. 150.
6. "Proceedings of a Board of Review.... " 24–25 June 1945, paras. 27, 29, 30, 32. Mediterranean Theater of Operations Report, "Participation of Negro Troops in the Post-War Military Establishment," 13 August 1945, Army General Forces Correspondence, 1942–1948, Record Group 337, National Archives, Suitland, MD.
7. Major General Edward Almond, "Approving Action of... Proceedings of the Board of Review...." 2 July 1945; "Proceedings of the Board of Review...." 24–25 June 1945, paras. 29 and 42, Record Group 337, National Archives, Suitland, MD.
8. Telephone Interview, John Runyon with Elliott V. Converse III, 26 September 1994.
9. Almond's Note to Chief of Staff, 16 June 1945, folder "Top Secret 92nd Infantry Division Combat Efficiency Analysis...."
10. There is additional evidence that Runyon's report was prepared on 1 July 1945, rather than on 12 April 1945. Both Almond's "Approving" letter and the division board's report refer to the fifteen appended reference documents by number. The 12 April 1945 version of Captain Runyon's report is identified as No. 11 in the listing of reference documents at the end of the

board's report. In the text of its report, the board employed parenthetical citations to refer to the fifteen appended supporting documents. In every instance that the board cited Runyon's report, the numerical citation was enclosed in separate parentheses placed next to the parentheses used to enclose the numbers of the other reference documents—a clear indication that the citations to Runyon's report were added after the board report had been completed. Further, the entries citing Runyon's report were made with a different typewriter, both in the board's report and Almond's "Approving" letter (the ribbon was evidently worn; the impression left by the keystrokes is lighter than the rest of the text).

    11. Major Paul Goodman, *A Fragment of Victory*, Army War College, Carlisle Barracks, PA, 1952, pp. 131–133.

    12. Interview of Vernon Baker by Joseph Galloway and Daniel Gibran on 28 August 1996.

    13. See *The Medal of Honor of the United States Army* (Washington, D.C.: U.S. Government Printing Office, 1948), p. 21.

    14. *Ibid.*

    15. Report of the General Board, United States Forces European Theater, "Awards and Decorations in a Theater of Operations," G-1 Section, Study Number 10, p. 8, Box 2, Reports of the General Board, USFET, Records of the U.S. Army, Dwight D. Eisenhower Library, Abilene, KS.

    16. Vernon J. Baker, *Lasting Valor: Story of the Only Living Black World War II Veteran to Earn America's Highest Distinction for Valor, the Medal of Honor* (Columbus, MS: Genesis Press, 1997), pp. 209–210.

    17. *Ibid.*, p. 219.

Chapter 5

    1. Telephone interview of Solace Wales by Daniel Gibran, followed by a facsimile document supplied by Interviewee from her home in Sommocolonia, Italy, on 27 April 2000.

    2. Interview of Mrs. Arlene Fox by Daniel Gibran on 7 November 1998 at her home in Houston, TX.

    3. *Ibid.*

    4. Letter of Lt. John Fox to daughter Sandra Marie Fox dated 15 December 1944, in the possession of Mrs. Arlene Fox at her home in Houston, TX. Copy of said letter obtained by author on 7 November 1998.

    5. William Wyatt, "On the Point with Lt. Fox," in 92nd Infantry Division's *Newsletter*, Summer, 1982, p.7.

    6. Ulysses Lee, *Employment of Negro Troops: United States Army in*

World War II (Washington, D.C.: U.S. Government Printing Office, 1966), p. 564.

7. See Edward Raymond, "Black Buffalo," *Field Artillery Journal*, January 1946, and Hondon Hargrove, *Buffalo Soldiers in Italy* (Jefferson, NC: McFarland, 1985), pp. 64–65.

8. Quoted in Jehu Hunter and Major Clark, *The Buffalo Division in World War II*, A Private Monograph published in March 1985, p. 55.

9. Interview of Brigadier General William Colbern by Major Bell Wiley, 2 July 1945, Almond Papers, United States Army Military History Institute, Carlisle Barracks, PA; Colonel Edward Raymond, Letter for Major Robert Roush (Military Awards Branch, U.S. Army Personnel Center), 18 September 1980, in First Lieutenant John R. Fox Individual Personnel Record, National Personnel Records Center.

10. Raymond, *Field Artillery Journal*, January 1946, p. 15.

11. Major General Edward Almond, Letter for Commanding Officer, 371st Infantry, "Deficiency in Combat Performance of Individuals and Units, 366th Infantry," 7 December 1944, folder "Report on the Operations of the 366th Regiment, Dec. 1944–Sept. 1945," Box 1362A, 92nd Infantry Division, World War II Operations Report, 1940–1948, RG 407, WNRC.

12. Captain C.H. Welch, Letter for Commanding General, 92nd Infantry Division, "Report of Investigation of Deficiency in Combat Performance of Officers and EM of Co "B," 366th Infantry Regiment," 23 December 1944, Box 13620B, 92nd Infantry Division, World War II Operations Report, 1940–1948, RG 407, WNRC.

13. Colonel William McCaffrey Statement, 19 June 1945, folder, "Report on the Operations of the 366th Infantry Regiment, Dec. 1944–Sept. 1945," Box 13620A, 92nd Infantry Division, World War II Operations Report, 1940–1948, RG 407, WNRC.

14. Major Stephen Rossetti, "Account of Battle of Sommocolonia as Related by Partisans," no date, in unmarked folder, Box 13620, 92nd Infantry Division, World War II Operations Reports, 1940–1948, RG 407, WNRC.

15. Interview of Colonel William McCaffrey by Joseph Galloway, 29 January 1997, Alexandria, VA.

16. Interview of Mrs. Arlene Fox by Daniel Gibran, 17 January 1997, Washington, D.C.

Chapter 6

1. Letter of Dr. C.F. Hopson to President of the United States, 13 March 1946, folder "291.2, 1 Jan 46–31 Mar 46, Box 799," Decimal 291.2, G-1

Decimal File, June 1946–48, Record Group 165, National Archives, Suitland, MD.

2. Public Information Division, United States Department of the Army, *The Medal of Honor of the United States Army* (Washington, D.C.: U.S. Government Printing, 1948), p. 3.

3. *Ibid.*

4. See Philip K. Robles, *United States Military Medals and Ribbons* (Rutland, VT: Charles Tuttle Company, 1971), p. 18.

5. *The Medal of Honor of the United States Army*, p. 21.

Chapter 7

1. Ulysses Lee, *The Employment of Negro Troops* (Washington, D.C.: U.S. Government Printing Office, 1966), pp. 328–330.

2. *Ibid.*, p. 347.

3. Interview of General William McCaffrey by Joseph Galloway, 29 January 1997, Alexandria, VA.

BIBLIOGRAPHY

Archives and Manuscript Collections

U.S. Army Center of Military History, Washington, DC

Unit Histories and Other Records Related to Black Soldiers

George C. Marshall Research Foundation Library, Lexington, VA

Papers of General George C. Marshall

U.S. Army Military History Institute, Carlisle Barracks, PA

Papers of Maj. Gen. Edward (Ned) Almond
Papers of Brig. Gen. Benjamin O. Davis, Sr.
Unit Histories and Other Records Related to the 92nd Infantry Division

The National Archives and Records Administration, College Park, MD

Record Group 107 (Records of the Secretary of War)
Record Group 165 (Records of the War Department)

Record Group 331 (Records of Allied Operational and Occupation Headquarters, World War II)
Record Group 332/492 (Records of the U.S. Army Theaters of War, World War II)
Record Group 337 (Records of the Army Ground Forces)
Record Group 338 (Records of U.S. Army Commands, 1942-) [Includes Awards Case Files]
Record Group 407 (Records of the Army Adjutant General) [Includes World War II Operational Reports, 1940-1948]

National Personnel Records Center, St. Louis, MO

Individual Personnel Records ("201" Files)
Awards Case Files

Interviews

Name	*Position*	*Date*
Baker, Vernon J.	Plt Ldr 92nd Infantry Division	28 Aug 96
Clark, Major	Btry Officer, 92nd Division Arty	25 Apr 94
Fox, Arlene	Widow of Lt. John Fox	07 Nov 98
Gibson, Truman K.	Civilian Aide, Sec of War	12 Mar 94
Hargrove, Hondon B.	Btry Officer, 92nd Infantry Division	13 Mar 94
Hunter, Jehu	Signal Officer, 92nd Infantry Division	14 Jan 97
McCaffrey, William	Chief of Staff, 92nd Infantry Division	29 Jan 97
Mitchell, Paren	Co Cmdr, 92nd Infantry Division	01 Mar 94
Solace Wales	Resident of Sommocolonia, Italy	27 Apr 00
Zachary, Otis	Btry Off, 92nd Infantry Division	10 Jul 94

Public Documents

U.S. Congress. Senate. Committee on Veteran's Affairs. Senate Committee Print No. 3, *Medal of Honor Recipients, 1863-1978*, 90th Congress, 1st Session. Washington, D.C.: U.S. Government Printing Office, 1979.

U.S. Department of the Army. Public Information Division. *The Medal of Honor of the United States Army*. Washington, D.C.: U.S. Government Printing Office, 1948.

Newspapers

Pittsburgh Courier, 1944-1945.
Stars and Stripes (European ed.), 1944-1945.
Washington Post, January 1997.

Articles and Books

Ambrose, Stephen E. "Blacks in the Army in Two World Wars," in Stephen E. Ambrose and James A. Barber, Jr., eds., *The Military in American Society*. New York: The Free Press, 1972.

Arnold, Thomas St. John. *Buffalo Soldiers: The 92nd Infantry Division and Reinforcements in World War II, 1942–1945*. Manhattan, KS: Sunflower University Press, 1990.

Baker, Vernon J. *Lasting Valor: Story of the Only Living Black World War II Veteran to Earn America's Highest Distinction for Valor, the Medal of Honor*. Columbus, MS: Genesis, 1997.

Blake, Joseph A. "The Congressional Medal of Honor in Three Wars." *Pacific Sociological Review*, April 1973: 166–176.

Braverman, Jordan. *To Hasten the Homecoming: How Americans Fought World War II Through the Media*. New York: Madison, 1996.

Bullard, Robert L. *Personalities and Reminiscences of the War*. New York: Doubleday, 1925.

Clark, Mark W. *Calculated Risk*. New York: Harper and Brothers, 1950.

Converse, Elliot V., Daniel Gibran, et al. *The Exclusion of Black Soldiers from the Medal of Honor in World War II*. Jefferson, NC: McFarland, 1997.

Cornish, Dudley. *The Sable Arm: Negro Troops in the Union Army, 1861–1865*. New York: Longmans, Green, 1956.

Dalfiume, Richard M. *Desegregation of the U.S. Armed Forces: Fighting on Two Fronts, 1939–1953*. Columbia: University of Missouri Press, 1969.

David, George F. "John Robert Fox: Congressional Medal of Honor." *The Kappa Alpha PSI Journal* (December 1996): 243–244.

Davis, Benjamin O., Jr. *Benjamin O. Davis, Jr.: American*. Washington, D.C.: Smithsonian Institution Press, 1991.

Fisher, Ernest F., Jr. *Cassino to the Alps [United States Army in World War II]*. Washington, D.C.: U.S. Government Printing Office, 1977.

Foner, Jack D. *Blacks and the Military in American History: A New Perspective*. New York: Praeger, 1974.

Gleim, Albert F., and George B Harris III. *Distinguished Service Cross Awards for World War II*. Revised Second Edition. Fort Myer, VA: Planchet, 1991.

Goodman, Paul. *A Fragment of Victory in Italy during World War II*. Carlisle Barracks, PA: Army War College, 1952.

Goodwin, Doris Kearns. *No Ordinary Time: The Home Front in World War II.* New York: Simon & Schuster, 1995.

Griffith, Robert K., Jr. *Men Wanted for the U.S. Army: America's Experience with an All-Volunteer Army Between the World Wars, 1919–1941.* New Haven, CT: Greenwood, 1982.

Hargrove, Hondon B. *Buffalo Soldiers in Italy: Black Americans in World War II.* Jefferson, NC: McFarland, 1985.

Hunter, Jehu, and Major Clark. *The Buffalo Division in World War II.* N.P.: By the Authors, 1985.

Jefferson, Robert F. *Making the Men of the 93rd: African-American Servicemen in the Years of the Great Depression and the Second World War, 1935–1947.* Doctoral Dissertation, Ann Arbor, MI: University of Michigan Dissertation Services, 1996.

Kenworthy, E.W. "The Case Against Army Segregation." *Annals of the American Academy of Political Science* 275 (May 1952): 28–29.

Lee, Ulysses. *The Employment of Negro Troops [United States Army in World War II].* Washington, D.C.: U.S. Government Printing Office, 1966.

Macgregor, Morris J., Jr. *Integration of the Armed Forces, 1940–1965 [Defense Studies Series].* Washington, DC: US Government Printing Office, 1981.

_____, Jr., et al. *American Military History [Army Historical Series].* Washington, D.C.: U.S. Government Printing Office, 1989.

Motley, Mary Penick, comp. and ed. *The Invisible Soldier: The Experience of Black Soldiers in World War II.* Detroit, MI: Wayne State University Press, 1975.

Murphy, Edward F. *Heroes of WWII.* New York: Ballantine, 1991.

Nalty, Bernard C. *Strength for the Fight: A History of Black Americans in the Military.* New York: The Free Press, 1986.

Osur, Alan M. *Blacks in the Army Air Forces During World War II: The Problem of Race Relations.* Washington, D.C.: U.S. Government Printing Office, 1977.

Perret, Geoffrey. *There's a War to Be Won: The United States Army in World War II.* New York: Random House, 1991.

Raymond, Edward A. "Black Buffalo." *The Field Artillery Journal* (January 1946): 14–17.

Robles, Philip K. *United States Military Awards and Ribbons.* Rutland, VT: Tuttle, 1971.

St. George, Andrew. "The Truth About the Negro Soldier." *Real: The Exciting Magazine for Men,* Vol. 9, No. 1 (November 1946): 12–16 and 65–72.

Stillman, Richard J. "The Role of the Negro in the U.S. Armed Forces, 1939–1968." *The Irish Defense Journal* (March 1969): 102–103.

Stimson, Henry L., and McGeorge Bundy. *On Active Service in Peace and War.* New York: Harper and Brothers, 1947.

Truscott, Lucian K., Jr. *Command Missions.* New York: Dutton, 1954.

INDEX

Abruzzi 52
Achilles' heel 13
Adriatic Sea 49
Advisory Committee on Negro Troop Policies 4
Africa Corps 11
Air Corps Tactical School (Maxwell Field) 30
Alabama 11
Alessandria 6
Alexandria, VA 176
Allied forces 6
Anderson, Marian 103
Apuane mountains 124
Aqua Prieta 16
Arab Muslims 54
Arizona 5
Arkansas 15
Armstrong, J. D. 102
Army Bureau of Public Relations 106
Army Chief of Chaplains 157
Army General Comprehensive Test 18
Army Ground Forces 17, 22
Army Intelligence Branch 30
Army Staff College 29
Army War College 3
Arno River 6
"Arsenal of Democracy" 12

Asians 118
Atterbury 14
Attila 53
Atlantic Ocean 15
Attucks, Crispus 1
Austro-Sardinian War 54

Balkans 11
Ballou, Charles 2
Band-aid approach (to Negro "problem" in Army) 164
Barbados 170
Barber, Colonel Frank 13
Barga 129; town of 133
Bebbio 130
Benewah Valley 116
Bethlehem 52
Bisbee 16
Bismarck 28
Blue Max 155
Bologna 74; vicinity of 77
Bosnia 166
Boston 1
Boys Town 94
Brazilian division 73
Breckinridge, KY 13, 14
British academic style 170
British Eighth Army 7
Brockton 138
Brooks, Eli 94

Brown, Lloyd 33, 34
Browning, George 28
Browning automatic rifle 84
Bryn Mawr 119
Buffalo Soldiers 21; history of 26
Bullard, Robert 2, 3
Byzantine Emperor 53

Caesar 52
Calcinaia 44
Camp Walters 94
Cannae 52
Cannon Company 128
Cape Town 51
Caribbean Development Bank 170
Carlisle Barracks 172
Carolina maneuvers 33
Carrara 43
Carrione Creek 75
Carter, Edward 148
Cash, John 84
Castle Aghinolfi 80, 82
Casual Camp 20, 23
Chandler, Jake 44
Charlemagne 54
Charles V, the Holy roman Emperor 54
Charles VIII of France 54
Charlottesville 28

195

196   Index

Chemical Mortar Battalion 76
Cheyenne 92
Chicago 174
China 29
Christmas 9
Cinquale Canal 58; analysis of 61; efforts to cross 60; north of 86
Clarinda, IA 92
Clark, Major 141
Clark, Mark 7, 33
Clay, Leroy 24
Clayton, McLorris 144
Clinton, President Bill 8; action by 149
Colbern, William 133
Columbus, Christopher 6; birthplace of 108
Combat Team 41
conceptual straightjacket 164
Congress 15
Congressional Medal of Honor 151
Converse, Elliott 144
Coreglia 130
Counts, Donald 87
court-martial hearings 24
Crittenberger, Willis 43
Croix de Guerre 2
Cumby, Bert 24

D-Day invasion 39
Dabney, Walter 135
Damocles 3; like the sword of 52
Davis, Benjamin 19; reported to 24
Decorations Board 152, 153
de' Medici family 111
Dorchester 126

East Room 155
Egyptian 11
Eisenhower, General 32, 64
El alamein 11
England 11
esprit 25; esprit de corps 48
estuary 72
Eternal City 49
Euro-centric superiority 21
Excelsior Hotel 109

Far East 107
Fernando 109

Field Artillery Journal 125
Fire Detection Center 132
Florence 111
Florentine plain 51
Fort Benning 32
Fort Devens 32, 126; chapel in 127
Fort Huachuca 5
Fort Leavenworth 29
Fort McClellan 11; men and officers from 14; special troops at 25
Fort McNair 29
Fort Ridley 93
Fortress Brigade 77
France 1, 2
Frankfurt 66
Franklin Park 126
Franks 54
Frigido River 75
Fry (community outside Fort Huachuca) 16

Galloway, Joseph: report by 148
Gandy, Charles 44
Garand rifles 99
Geiger Field 97
Genoa 6
George Marshall Library 146
Georgia 33
Germans 7; German Army 6
Gibbon, Edward 53
Gibson, Edwin 27
Gibson, Truman 4, 5
Goodman, Paul 48
Gothic Line 8
Great St. Bernard 54
Great Wall 29
Greece 52
Green, Carl 93
Green Line Defense 75
Green Machine 93
Grenada 166
Griffith, Robert 144
Gruenther, Alfred 66
Gulf of Genoa 50

Hall, Admiral 31
Halsey, Admiral 31
Hampton Roads 41
Hannibal 52
Hapsburgs 54
Hargrove, Hondon 21
Harrod, Dennette 62

Hasie (pet name for Vernon Baker) 119
Hawaii 119
Hayden Lake 121
hazing 29
Highway 12 46
Hispanics 118
Hitler's aggression 12
Hollywood 111
Holy Land 54
Hopson, C. F. 141
Howard University 144
Hunter, Jehu 141

Iceland 11
Idaho: isolated cottage in 8
Imperial Rome 52
Indian Campaigns 153
Indian Division 132
Indian Wars 142
Indiana 14
Intelligence Branch 30
Israel, enemies of 139
Italian partisans 129

Jacob (ship) 107
Japan 29
Japanese-American Regiment 65
Jenkins, Graham 130
Jim Crow laws 21
Johns Hopkins University 35
Johnson, Henry 2
Joint Chiefs of Staff 166
Joint Resolution of Congress 177
Justinian, Emperor 53

malingering 19
Marengo 28, 54
Marga River 75
Marina di Pisa 51
Marine Corps 166
Marshall, General 4, 34, 35
Maryland 137
Mason-Dixon Line 28
Massa 6, 7
Maxwell Field 30
McCaffrey, William 68
McCarthy era 148
McCloy, John J. 4
McKinney, Gene 157
McNair, General 33
McNarney, Joseph 102

Index

Medal of Honor Roll 152
Memorial Field 107
Mexico 30
micro-management 70
Miles, General 32
Mineral Wells 94
Mitchell, Parren 23
Molise 52
Mongolia 29
Monroe Doctrine 30
Monte Rosa Division 77
Montgomery 30
Montignoso 75
Morgan State University 144
Mount Albano 44
Mount Altissimo 43
Mount Brugiana 75
Mount Cauala 56
Mount Folgorito 59
Mount Pisano 44
Mount Strettoia 57
Murphy, Lieutenant Colonel 85
Mussolini 129, 130

Naco 16
Napoleon 28
National Archives 137
National Guard 2
Native Americans 118
Naval War College 31
Nazis 11; war machine 12
Negro Interest Section 106
Negro race 103
New Guinea 107
New York 32
New York Times 45
Newport 31
Newport News 99
Nimitz, Admiral 31
Nogales 16
Normandy 39
North Africa 4
North Carolina State University 170
Notestein, James 102

Observation Post No. 1 78
Odoacer (Germanic leader) 53
Officer Candidate School 96
Ohio 126
Oklahoma 93
Old Post 95
Operation Craftsman 74

Operation Fourth Team 63
Operation Second Wind 40
operational architecture 162
Organ, Kenny 116
Ostrogoths 53

Pacific command 107
Pacific Theater 98
Page County 27
Panama 166
Panzer Grenadier Division 7
Papal States 54
Paquet, Anthony 154
Parmignola River 75
Patton, General 31
Pearl Harbor 33
Pennsylvania 119
Pentagon 120
Pershing, General 29
Persian Gulf War 166
Pesaro 43
Phelan, John 58
Philippines 29, 142
Pico, Fretter 133
Pietrasanta 79
Pisa 6
Pistoia 43
Po River Valley 7, 28
Pompey 52
Pontedera 6
Porlock Harbor 107
Porta Ridge 77; objective on 81
Powell, Colin 155
Punic Wars 52
Punta Bianca 59; gunfire from 62; low hills of 72

Quartermaster Corps 111
Querceta 79

Rainbow Coalition 67
Red Cross 113, 115
Reno River 43; east of 73
Request for Proposal (RFP) 143
Rheims 90
Rhode Island 31
Rivers, Ruben 147, 156
Roberts, Needham 2
Robinson, AR 15
Rome 49; Roman Empire 49
Rommel 11

ROTC program 126
Roush, Robert 137
Rowney, Edward 23, 58
Rubicon 52
Runyon, John 81
Russia 11
Ryder, Charles 32

Sabine Hills 51
St. Augustine College 170
St. Joe River 115
St. Maries 8
Sam Marco Division 77
Samnite Wars 52
Samson (Biblical story) 139
San Francisco 29
Sand Point 121
Saracens 54
Sardinia 49
Schussel, Christian 154
Selective Service Act 21
Sera River 56
Seravezza 56
Serchio Valley 7, 9, 43
Shannon, John 143, 155
Shatto, Harry 147
Shaw, Talbert 171
Shaw University (Raleigh, NC) 143
Shea, Donald W. 157
Sherman, Raymond 41, 47
Sicily 49
Solomon Islands 5
Somalia 166
Sommocolonia 123, 124; attack on 128–133
South Africa 51
Spain 52; in the conflict with 142
Spanish-American War 153
Sparks, Chauncey 13
Spokane 97
Spring Offensive 24
Stalingrad 11
Statement of Work 143
Stimson, Henry 4
Stonewall Jackson 13; imposing statue of 28
Strait of Messina 49
Suitland 137
Swanson, Claude 28
Sweden 170

Tactical Air Command 58

Theodoric (Teutonic chieftain) 53
Thomas, Charles 158
Tiber 51
Tombstone, AZ 16
Truman, Harry 141
Truscott, Lucian 59, 61, 63
Turin 6
Tyrrhenian Sea 49

United States Army Institute of Military History 145
United States Military Academy 27

University of North Carolina, Chapel Hill 144
Ushio 100
U. S. News & World Report 148
USS *Mariposa* 99

Venice 52
Viareggio 55, 92
Victoria Cross 151
Vietinghoff, Heinrich Von 91
Vietnam War 153
Virginia Military Academy 28
Visigoths 53

Washington, Booker T. 103
Watson, George 107, 157; kin of 150
Wehrmacht 8, 73
West, Togo D. 148; Secretary of the Army 155
West Point 27, 28, 32
West Virginia 141
White House 138
Wilberforce University 126
Wilder, A. D. 102
Williams, David 156
Wyoming 92

Zachary, Otis 139, 140

www.ingramcontent.com/pod-product-compliance
Ingram Content Group UK Ltd.
Pitfield, Milton Keynes, MK11 3LW, UK
UKHW042007140426
5217IPUK00015B/1030